F.A.C.T.S.

(Faith And Commitment Through Scripture)

Other Books in This Series:

Book 2: Romans, Colossians, Philemon, Ephesians, & Philippians

Book 3: Luke, Mark

Book 4: Acts, 1 Peter

Book 5: 1 Timothy, Titus, Matthew

Book 6: 2 Timothy, 2 Peter, Hebrews, Jude

Book 7: John, 1 John, 2 John, 3 John, Revelation

F.A.C.T.S.

(Faith And Commitment Through Scripture)

A Bible Study Series

BOOK 1

Joanne Liggan

Copyright © 2017 Joanne Liggan

All rights reserved.

ISBN-10: 1542814782
ISBN-13: 978-1542814782

Thank you to Lynn Hite, Thelma Reid, and the late Ann
Blake for starting me on this path;

and

A special thank you to my consultants/editors,
Rev. Rebekah Johns, Sharon Jones, and
Celie Thomas, for encouraging me to continue this journey
whenever I considered giving up.

JOANNE LIGGAN

F.A.C.T.S.

CONTENTS

Preface	vii
Introduction	1
Book of James	3
Letters to the Thessalonians	45
Picture of Paul of Tarsus	49
Letter to the Galatians	91
Map of Galatia	92
Letters to the Corinthians	137
Bibliography	295
About the Author	299

Preface

F.A.C.T.S.

F.A.C.T.S. is an acronym for Faith And Commitment Through Scripture. This acronym was chosen as the title of this series for a couple of reasons. First, it is my hope all readers will be strengthened in their faith and their commitment to Christ as they study the scriptures. And secondly, the Bible is a book of facts, not conjecture. It contains facts about the history of the world and its people, as well as facts of what is to come. A quote from Sgt. Joe Friday (played by Jack Webb in an old show called Dragnet, which ran from 1949 on radio to 1970 on TV) comes to mind—"Just the facts, ma'am." All he wanted were the facts, or the "truth." The goal for this study is to give readers "the facts" as presented by the holy scriptures.

NOTE FROM THE AUTHOR

The scriptures were written for all of God's people, not only the theologians or well-educated people. I am a Christian who believes in the Holy Spirit's ability to guide us as we study God's Word. During the writing of these study guides, I prayed for His guidance and attempted to focus on the written Word and the clear intention therein.

The scriptures were written through the inspiration and guidance of the Holy Spirit. We have a duty to read and interpret them in the same way—with the inspiration and guidance of the Holy Spirit. If we attempt to understand them on our own, we will fail. So before beginning this study, please pray for the Holy Spirit to help you understand and reveal to you the truth. No matter where we are in our spiritual journey, God reveals to us according to our ability to comprehend. The more we study and grow, the more He reveals.

On February 4, 2002, a few friends gathered in my home to begin a Bible study. It is difficult to believe that was so many years ago! These study guides are the product of that sown little seedling. What began as a study for a few friends has now grown, first into a blog, and now in book form, reaching many throughout the world. How amazing!

My prayer is for God to use this ministry to reach at least one lost soul and create a hunger within that person so he/she will accept Christ as his/her personal Savior. Furthermore, I pray the Christians who read my blog or study guides will grow in their knowledge of the Word and grow stronger as Christians so they can be effective witnesses for Christ to bring others into God's family.

"Just as rain water comes down in drops and forms rivers, so with the Scriptures: one studies a bit today and some more tomorrow, until in time the understanding becomes like a flowing stream."— Song of Songs Midrash Rabbah 2:8, as quoted in Lois Tuerberg's *Walking in the Dust of Rabbi Jesus*.

Introduction

In this series of study guides of God's Holy Word, we will begin with the book of James, believed by some to be the first book of the New Testament written, and work our way through to the last book written. We will study the period of history and the writers and their particular situations, focusing on why they wrote the letters, to whom they wrote them, and take what they wrote in context with what was going on during that time period. This will help us understand the writings more thoroughly and be sure nothing is taken out of context.

Quoting of verses has purposely been omitted within the context of these books. Readers should not rely solely on this study guide. It is to be used in conjunction with the Bible. The chapters and verses are listed for readers to look up and read for themselves in the hopes it will assist them in learning where to find the scriptures, helping them to become more familiar and more comfortable with God's Word. Our Bible should be our closest and dearest friend. The more we open it and read it, the closer we will feel to our Lord and Savior.

2 Peter 1:20-21 *"Above all, you must understand, that no prophecy of Scripture came about by the prophet's own interpretation. For prophecy never had its origin in the will of man, but men spoke from God as they were carried along by the Holy Spirit."*

1 Corinthians 2:13 *"This is what we speak, not in words taught us by human wisdom, but in words taught by the Spirit, expressing spiritual truths in spiritual words."*

2 Timothy 3:16-17 *"All Scripture is God-breathed and is useful for teaching, rebuking, correcting and training in righteousness, so that the man of God may be thoroughly equipped for every good work."*

Proverbs 30:5-6 *"Every word of God is flawless; He is a shield to those who take refuge in Him. Do not add to His words, or He will rebuke you and prove you a liar."*

Psalm 119:130 *"The unfolding of your words gives light; it gives understanding to the simple."*

Colossians 3:16 *"Let the word of Christ dwell in you richly as you teach and admonish one another with all wisdom…"*

Luke 11:28 *"He (Jesus) replied, 'Blessed rather are those who hear the word of God and obey it."*

F.A.C.T.S.

The Book of

JAMES

JOANNE LIGGAN

James, The Brother Of Jesus & Author Of The Book Of James

Let's begin at the beginning. As far as historians can tell, the first New Testament letter written was either 1 Thessalonians, written by Paul, or the Book of James, penned by none other than the brother of Jesus. Both letters were written very close together in 49 or 50 A.D. For our purposes, we will begin with James. We'll begin by learning more about the man before we delve into his letter.

Jesus walked this earth, taught those He encountered, and was crucified, but the only way anyone knew anything about His teachings were through actual witnesses and word of mouth. The only Scriptures the churches had were the scrolls we know as the Old Testament.

After Jesus's death and resurrection, two of His brothers, James and Jude, wrote letters to the churches regarding issues Christians were facing, and the churches kept the letters for all to read. These letters, along with others, became what we now know as our New Testament.

How do we know it was James, Jesus's brother, who wrote this letter?

There are four men in the New Testament with the name James:
1. There was an apostle named James, Son of Zebedee and Salome and the brother of John. This apostle could not have written this letter because it was written in 49 AD, or soon thereafter, and he died in 44 AD, four years earlier.
2. Another apostle was James the Less, Son of Alphaeus. As his name indicates, this apostle did not have the position in society to have the influence the writer of this letter must have had.
3. The third James is the father of Judas the apostle, and nothing else is ever mentioned about him, so he probably was not well-known enough to speak with the authority indicated by the author.
4. And the other James mentioned in the New Testament is the brother of Jesus. This James was recognized as the leading Overseer of the Judean Church. He was very influential both among the Jews and within the Church.

NOTE: There is some controversy regarding James actually being the brother of Jesus. This is mainly due to the Catholic church insisting Mary remained a perpetual virgin even after Jesus's birth. However, it is widely accepted among Protestants that Mary had other children with Joseph after Jesus was born, including James, Joseph, Simon, and Judas, as well as sisters whose names are not given. These are mentioned in Mark 6:3 and again in Matthew 13:53-56.

The Book of James was written in excellent Greek, making it clear the writer was very well educated. Among the four listed above, the brother of Jesus would have been the only one well educated in the Greek language.

Also, the author writes with an air of authority and refers to himself as 'the Lord's brother'. Although the Greek term (adelphos) [ad el fos'] means 'brother', it can also mean 'cousin' or 'kinsman'. But in this case it is believed to actually mean 'brother' or 'sibling'. Usually when indicating 'brotherhood' or 'brethren', the Greek used the word adelphotes [ad el fot' ace], not adelphos.

How much do we know about Jesus's brother, James?

Following are some of the scriptures that tell us about him.

Read Mark 6:3

This verse refers to Jesus, mentioning his mother and his siblings. It was the custom at that time to list brothers from the oldest to the youngest. Since his name is first on the list, it is believed he was the oldest of the four brothers of Jesus.

Read John 7:2-5

These verses show his brothers mocking him. Before the resurrection, Jesus's brothers did not believe Him to be God's Son and didn't understand His mission. They challenged Him concerning His mission.

I suppose it would be difficult to believe your sibling is the Son of God. You tend to see your brothers and sisters as equal to yourself, so imagine if one of them is claiming to be the Messiah! It must have been a huge pill for them to swallow.

Read 1 Corinthians 15:7

James was among those to whom Christ appeared after his resurrection.

Read Acts 1:13-14

James was also present at the meeting of the disciples after the resurrection.

When Jesus arose and appeared before him, it must have been very convincing! It's hard to deny someone who has just risen from the dead.

How do we know James was well-known and respected?

We know Paul respected him, for he chose to consult him, and only him, soon after his conversion.

Read Galatians 1:19

Paul visited James in Jerusalem soon after his conversion around 35 AD. Paul also referred to James as the 'pillar' of the church.

Read Galatians 2:9

Peter thought highly of him. Peter reported to him upon his release from prison around 44 AD.

Read Acts 12:17

James was very influential both among the Jews and in the Church. He was a very strict Jew himself, but wrote this tolerant letter to converted Jewish Christians sometime between 48 AD and 51 AD. He was probably (although we cannot be certain) between 45 and 50 years old when he penned this letter. He endorsed Paul's Gentile work, but was himself mainly concerned with Jews. His life's work was to win Jews, and 'smooth their passage to Christianity'.

About the year 49 AD, James became chairman of the Council of the Church in Jerusalem. At that time, there was a strong party of Jews that opposed welcoming Gentiles because they did not observe the Laws of Moses. James was well respected by both Jews and Christians because he was very 'politically correct' for his time and was able to negotiate on both sides of the issue between Jews and Gentiles.

Read Acts 15:12-29

James ruled that Pagans who turned to God were to abstain from food offered to idols, from the meat of strangled animals, and also from fornication. No other rules were imposed on Gentiles, which made them happy. And Jews felt vindicated because the Gentiles were held to some of their Laws.

Paul sought his advice and respected him enough to follow that advice.

Read Acts 21:18-26

Read Luke 24:10

When Christ was crucified, notice how Mary was identified as the *"mother of James"* rather than the mother of Jesus. And in ***Jude 1,*** Jude identified himself as *'a servant of Jesus Christ and a brother of James'*.

The fact that he called himself *'a servant of Jesus Christ'* only goes to show he was convinced Jesus was God's Son. He was not equal to Jesus, that's why he did not say he was His brother.

The fact that Mary and Jude identified themselves with James, but not as relatives of Jesus, was a way of placing Christ above them rather than equal to them. But to better clarify who he was, Jude claimed James as his brother because James was so well-known.

Many scholars have tried to claim James was actually from a former marriage of Joseph's and wasn't truly a brother of Jesus, but this verse, among many others, clearly states Mary was the mother of James, putting their theory to rest.

Read 1 Corinthians 9:5

This verse indicates James was probably married and had his wife accompany him on his travels.

That's what the *Scriptures* tell us about James. *Historians* tell us James became known by the Jews as 'James the Just' because of his strict observance of the law. He was known as an unusually good man who spent so much time on his knees in prayer they became hard and callous like a camel's knees.

In order to follow the next section, you should know who the players are:

The ***Sanhedrin*** were the high court of the Jewish laws. They were called on to settle disputes and make decisions.

The ***Scribes*** were writers of the laws.

The ***Pharisees*** were among the strongest religious organizations during the time of Christ. They were mostly middle class and were the 'people's party'.

By 62 AD Jews were embracing Christianity in large numbers. Ananus, the High Priest, and the Scribes (lawmakers) and Pharisees (strong religious political party), assembled the Sanhedrin (high court) and commanded James, "the brother of Jesus who was called Christ", to proclaim from one of the galleries of the Temple that Jesus was ***not*** the Messiah. Instead, James cried out that Jesus was the Son of God and Judge of the World.

Then his enraged enemies hurled him to the ground and stoned him until one of them ended his sufferings with a club while he was on his knees praying, "Father, forgive them, they know not what they do." So history tells us James died a martyr, killed by a mob in Jerusalem.

Shortly thereafter, about 70 AD, the Roman army destroyed Jerusalem.

Now that we know a little bit about the man who wrote this letter, let's see what this respected and wise man has to tell us.

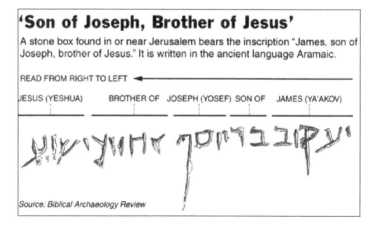

James – Chapter 1

The main theme of this letter is 'if we are true followers of Christ, we will show it by acting like Christians'. He gives practical advice on such things as anger, arguing, showing partiality, keeping the tongue under control, bragging, patience and prayer. If we could master all of these, just imagine the effect we could have on the world.

Read James 1:1

First James identifies himself – James, servant of God and of the Lord Jesus Christ. As mentioned previously, he did not call himself the brother of Jesus because he did not want to put himself on the same level as the Messiah. He made it clear he was a servant of the Lord.

Then he identifies to whom he's writing – the 12 tribes of Israel, who have, by this time, been scattered throughout the different nations.

(These are the 12 tribes of Israel as shown in Genesis 49) Sons of Jacob: Reuben, Simeon, Levi, Judah, Zebulun, Issachar, Dan, Gad, Asher, Naphtali, Joseph, Benjamin

What caused the 12 tribes to be spread out among the nations?

They had been persecuted and chased from place to place in search of safety and acceptance. There were thriving Jewish-Christian communities through Rome, Alexandria, Cyprus and cities in Greece and Asia Minor. But these communities did not have the support of established Christian churches, so James wrote to them to encourage them and explain to them the difference between 'religion' and 'true faith'.

Read James 1:2-4

James addresses the readers as brothers 15 times during this letter – which shows how much he cares for them.

James explains the attitude we should have toward trials. Notice he doesn't say IF you face trials, but "whenever you do." We learn perseverance when our faith is tested which in turn causes us to mature as Christians. We can't really know the depth of our character until we see how we react under pressure. It's easy to be kind to others when everything is going well, but what about when others are treating us unfairly? It's through trials and suffering we develop Christian character. So knowing that these trials are going to help us grow stronger as Christians, we should rejoice when we face these extra pressures in our lives.

The point is not to pretend to be happy about your pain and suffering, but to have a positive outlook about what will be gained by the experience. Look at it as an opportunity for growth.

Read James 1:5

The 'wisdom' James is speaking of here is insight into God's wisdom, not textbook learning. We should seek sound judgment about the practical things of daily life so as to live as a Christian should. Prayer will help us attain such wisdom. When we have difficult decisions to make, we should pray for God's wisdom to make the right choices.

God answers prayer generously. All you have to do is ask. God does not debate whether you are worthy of the wisdom, but gives to anyone who asks.

There is only ONE proviso or condition:

Read James 1:6-8

What effect does doubt have on a person when he or she prays? His words are empty and meaningless. He has no direction, but can be steered by a whim. His mind is changeable and his prayers are worthless because he still feels unsettled and restless, tossed about like the waves of the sea.

How often have you prayed for something, but then continued to worry about it? Then you felt the need to pray for it again later because you hadn't been sincere in your belief the first time.

So the condition for God to answer your prayers is for you to not have doubts, but believe that He will answer in His wisdom and in His own time. If you truly believe God will answer your prayers, you won't worry anymore once you've prayed about something, because you will have the assurance that it is in God's hands.

Read James 1:9-11

On the surface it looks like James is simply saying, if you are poor, be glad because your poverty will cause you to face trials that will help you grow into a strong Christian. But his deeper meaning is that you possess a position in God's Kingdom that is not judged by your earthly wealth. Although you may be overlooked by earthly society, you will not be overlooked by God.

If you are rich, you should remember that you are no better in God's Kingdom because of your earthly wealth. Remember, your riches will not save you from aging and dying. As the rich man concentrates on his earthly position and wealth, his soul could wither away. We find true wealth by developing our spiritual life, not by increasing our financial assets.

So this is a solemn reminder that our status in Eternity should be our main concern, not our status here on earth.

Read James 1:12

God promises eternal life to persecuted Christians.

Read James 1:13-15

God never tempts us. He cannot be tempted because He in His very nature is Holy & there is nothing in Him for sin to appeal to – nor does He tempt anyone.

Temptation comes from our own evil desires. Temptation begins with an evil thought. It becomes sin when we dwell on that thought and allow it to become an action.
("temptation gives birth to sin and sin gives birth to death"). The wages of sin is death.

God might test us, but never tempt us. He only tests us to confirm our faith or prove our commitment. (see Deut. 8:2-5)

What is the difference between tempting and testing?

Temptation is an enticement to sin.

Testing is an examination to determine quality, value, or character.

Temptation involves some form of evil or sinfulness.

God cannot be a part of anything evil or sinful. Any testing from God does not involve evil or sin, but may involve some type of hardship such as illness or other human trials. Christ was 'tempted' by Satan on the mount. The disciples were 'tested' by the persecution they suffered.

Temptation will often come after a high point in our spiritual lives or ministries. Remember that Satan chooses the times for his attacks, so be on guard at all times.

When you face trials, first make sure you haven't brought them on yourself through sin or unwise choices. If you find no sin to confess or unwise behavior to change, then ask God to strengthen you for your test.

God doesn't place the temptation in front of us, but He WILL watch to see how we respond to it. We have free will to choose the sin or to choose righteousness. God will only step in to remove the temptation from us if we ask Him.

Read James 1:16-18

Every good and perfect gift is from God. God is described here as the Father of lights (Creator of the heavenly bodies, which give light to the earth), but, unlike the shadows from these heavenly lights, God does not change.

God gives us birth through His Word of Truth, which is the Gospel. 'Birth' is not a reference to creation, but to regeneration, renewal or rebirth, as seen in John 3:3-8.

'First fruits' – Just as the first sheaf of harvest was an indication that the entire harvest was to follow, so the early Christians were an indication that a great number of people would eventually be born again.

Read James 1:19-21

First—'Keep your ears open and your mouth shut'. When we talk too much and listen too little, we are communicating to others that we think our ideas are more important than theirs. So we need to put a mental stopwatch on our conversations and keep track of how much we talk and listen. Don't you find yourself drawn to people who are open to hearing your ideas rather than those who treat you as if what you say doesn't matter?

Second—Keep your anger in check – anger does not encourage righteousness. A lot of our anger comes from selfishness. 'I am hurt.' Or 'I'm being treated unjustly.' We should become angry if others are being hurt, but not when we fail to win an argument or are offended or neglected. Selfish anger never helps anyone.

Anger is not a sin. It is a normal human emotion. However, it is a very powerful one, which can easily cause us to sin. Much of our anger is justified. We should become angry over injustice, such as the Holocaust or other horrible acts against mankind or travesties against God. Even Jesus became angry. Remember when he upended tables of the money-changers in the temple? (This story is found in John 2:13-23.)

Next—Rid yourself of immorality and evil and Accept the "Word" planted in you – "Word of God."

Read James 1:22-25

We develop our 'identity as a Christian' through obedience to the Word. James compares it to looking into a mirror and then walking away and forgetting what you looked like. The Word is the mirror we should look into to see if we look like a Christian or not.

Remember, when James wrote this, the only "scripture" they had was the Torah. The "Word" James mentions here is not our Holy Scriptures, but the "Truth" planted in us through Jesus, the Christ, the Messiah. James calls followers of Christ to trust in this Word (Jesus).

Today, we have the scriptures to help us understand how we should live and teach us what Jesus wanted us to be. We can measure the effect of our Bible study time by how it changes our actions. If our behavior and attitudes haven't changed, then we are not putting into action the things we're studying.

"perfect law" – moral and ethical teachings of Christianity

The word "perfect" here means "complete". The Messiah came to make the Torah complete. He fulfilled the Law and gave us the new covenant we know as Christianity.

"freedom" – the Torah, or old law, made men a slave to sin. But Christians enjoy the joyous freedom to be that which we were created to be. We are free to serve God out of love, not from the slavish obedience of the Law.

Read James 1:26-27

"religious" refers to outward acts of religion

Once again, James warns us to keep our tongues under control. If we don't, our other goodly acts will be worthless.

How could our tongue cancel out all of our other good and moral acts?

The world will see us as hypocrites. Our witness for Christ is eclipsed, or blocked out, by our harsh or offensive words.

Acts God accepts as pure and faultless are:

1. Looking after orphans and widows: In the first century, when this was written, orphans and widows had very little means of support. Unless a family member was willing to care for them, they had to resort to begging, selling themselves as slaves, or starving. By caring for these people, the church put God's Word into practice. When we give without hope of receiving in return, we show what it means to serve others.

2. Keep yourself from being polluted by the world. The world measures worth by money, power and pleasure. True faith means nothing if our lives are contaminated with these values.

"Life is 10 percent of what happens to you and 90 percent of how you respond to what happens to you."
--Charles R. Swindoll

James – Chapter 2

(In this chapter, James' continues with his theme on the development of Christian behavior)

Acts 2:45 tells us *"Selling their possessions and goods, they gave to anyone as he had need."*

And in Acts 4:34-35, we find *"There were no needy persons among them. For from time to time those who owned lands or houses sold them, brought the money from the sales and put it at the apostles' feet, and it was distributed to anyone as he had need."*

These verses explain how the first century church members took care of each other. If someone was in need, the other members of the church would make sure their needs were met.

Read James 2:1-5

Believers should not show favoritism because God doesn't show any favoritism. Christians should have equal respect for all people.

In verse 2, the word translated as '*meeting*' was actually the Greek term sunagoge (soon-ag-o-gay´) and is the origin of the English word 'synagogue'. Its literal meaning in Greek was "a bringing together" and was used in the NT as "an assembly of Christian Jews." This is how we know James was writing to converted Jews. They were still meeting in their synagogue.

The Judean church must have been showing a lot of favoritism to the rich and shunning the poor. James is trying to explain to them this is not the way Christians should act. To do so, he reminds them that showing favoritism is evil. The Jews, even prior to conversion, were familiar with this idea.

Deuteronomy 1:17 says *"Do not show partiality in judging; hear both small and great alike. Do not be afraid of any man, for judgment belongs to God. Bring me any case too hard for you, and I will hear it."*

So James is not telling them anything new here, just reminding them of how they should treat people.

We all know people who are 'religious' without being true Christians. The people James was writing to were very religious, but their actions didn't portray the love of God. We have to ask ourselves if our actions, both within the church and outside of the church, will portray God's love to others.

Read James 2:6-8

"royal law": called the 'royal' law because it is the supreme law that is the source of all other laws governing human relationships. The crux of the "royal law" is love; "Love your neighbor as yourself."

Again, James refers to laws with which the Jewish people are already familiar. This is one of the laws handed down to Moses and written in the Leviticus 19:18: *"'Do not seek revenge or bear a grudge against one of your people, but love your neighbor as yourself. I am the LORD.' "*

Read Luke 10:25-37

This parable is a perfect illustration of the "royal law."

For James, sin is violating the royal law of love, not breaking God's commandments. For let's face it, who among us can honestly keep them all! God's judgment will be without mercy toward those who show no mercy themselves. True Christianity has more to do with love than with obeying the Law. We are clearly told in 1 Corinthians 13:13, *"Now faith, hope, and love abide, but the greatest of these is love."*

Read James 2:9-11

The law is the expression of the character and will of God, therefore to break one law is to violate God's will and thus is equal to breaking all of the laws. He gave us the Law so we would know His boundaries and to define right from wrong on His terms. On human terms, we tend to measure sins as small sins and great sins. But sin is sin. To sin means we've offended God and merit His judgment. God, in His infinite wisdom, realizes humans are incapable of living lives free of sin. It is impossible for anyone to be in a relationship with God by keeping all of the commandments. That is why he sent His Son. Through Christ, we are released from the shackles of the Law, and are to live our lives through trust in Christ and love of God and our fellow man. The Law is a guideline, not our judgment.

Read James 2:12-13

We will all stand before the judgment seat of Christ.

2 Corinthians 5:10 tells us *"For we must all appear before the judgment seat of Christ, that each one may receive what is due him for the things done while in the body, whether good or bad."*

And in Revelation 22:12, we read *"Behold, I am coming soon! My reward is with me, and I will give to everyone according to what he has done."*

And finally, 1 Corinthians 3:12-15 tells us *"If any man builds on this foundation using gold, silver, costly stones, wood, hay or straw, his work will be shown for what it is, because the Day will bring it to light. It will be revealed with fire, and the fire will test the quality of each man's work. If what he has built survives, he will receive his reward. If it is burned up, he will suffer loss; he himself will be saved, but only as one escaping through the flames."*

Take special note of the last verse here and the good imagery. So even though you may be saved from the eternal fire, you may escape it by the skin of your teeth, depending upon how you perform as a Christian. If we are merciful to others, God will be merciful to us on the day of our judgment.

Read James 2:14

On the surface, this seems to contradict Paul's doctrine that we are saved by faith and not by works, but it actually supplements Paul's teachings. We know by Acts 15:13-29 and 21:17-26 that Paul and James worked together. The difference was that Paul was preaching to the Gentiles and James was preaching to the Jews. These two groups had different ideas about what was acceptable. So Paul and James had to adapt the way they taught so that each group would accept this new Christianity. Paul preached Faith as the basis of salvation, but insisted that this faith would change the kind of life we would want to live. James was preaching to Jews who had already accepted Paul's doctrine of faith but were still not living right, telling them that such faith was no faith at all. True faith would bring about change in their lives.

Having 'faith' in something can merely mean to have an intellectual acceptance of certain truths, but not necessarily true faith in Christ as Savior. James is distinguishing between the two here. Faith without deeds is NOT true faith in Christ. Genuine faith will produce good deeds, and it is only this kind of faith in Jesus Christ that will bring salvation.

Read James 2:15-17

Faith without good deeds, or a change in our attitude, is compared to pretending to care about others or showing fake consideration. If you really care about someone and know they are in need, would you just wish them well and continue on your way, leaving them to fend for themselves? Not if you really cared about them! You would see to it that they had all they needed before you left them. In the same way, if you have true faith, you will live a more pure life and not continue on in your old habits.

Read James 2:18-19

The Jews tried to say their faith was different from the Gentiles. Some people did good deeds, and others had faith. James is explaining to them there is no way to prove you have faith except by your deeds. If you have faith, you will do good deeds. If you don't do good deeds, your faith is dead.

James points out here that even the demons believe in one God, and they shudder.

Why do they shudder? Because they know God's power and fear Him. The demons know and believe in God, but belief alone does not warrant salvation.

Faith and belief are two separate things. We can believe something exists without liking it or allowing it to affect us. So believing in Christ is not enough. We must have the kind of faith that brings about a transformation in our lives.

James is not saying deeds save you. He is simply pointing out that if you have true faith, the deeds will take care of themselves. Deeds are evidence of our faith.

Galatians 5:6 says *"For in Christ Jesus neither circumcision nor uncircumcision has any value. The only thing that counts is faith expressing itself through love."*

Faith that saves produces deeds of love.

Read James 2:20-22

Here James gives an example of faith revealing itself through deeds. Imagine how much faith, or trust, Abraham had in God for him to be willing to sacrifice his young son!

Read James 2:23

Because of his faith, Abraham was called "God's friend." This is an expression of complete and total acceptance.

Read James 2:24

If taken out of context, this verse seems to contradict our belief in being saved through our faith and not by our deeds. But once again, James is stressing how true faith will cause good deeds. If your actions don't show love, your faith is not real, but merely an intellectual acceptance of certain truths. Your head tells you it's true, but your heart hasn't truly absorbed it. This is what the Bible refers to as 'hardened hearts'. Although you believe in the truth of the Gospel, rather than allow this truth to change you, you 'harden your heart' against it and continue in your own will.

Hebrews 3:8-9 says *"do not harden your hearts as you did in the rebellion, during the time of testing in the desert, where your fathers tested and tried me and for forty years saw what I did."*

When the Israelites were wandering around in the desert, they knew God. They believed in Him because they saw all the things He was doing for them. Yet they turned against Him. They had an intellectual faith that He existed and could help them, yet they didn't have whole-hearted trust in Him enough to obey Him. Their faith was dead.

Read James 2:25

Here James is not approving of Rahab's occupation, but is pointing out that even this unrighteous woman was saved by grace through her trust in God, which caused her to do good deeds and changed her destiny.

Read James 2:26

In summary, what good is the body without the spirit? It is empty and dead. The same is true about faith without deeds.

Which is easier for you – talking about your faith with others, or demonstrating love toward them? Which will get the better response from them? If you demonstrate your love to others, this will show them your faith. Talk is cheap—actions speak louder than words.

James – Chapter 3

With which part of the body can we--without much effort--do the most harm to others?

Read James 3:1-6

Teaching was a highly valued and respected profession in Jewish culture, and many Jews who embraced Christianity wanted to become teachers. James is simply warning them that, although it is good to aspire to teach, it is a great responsibility.

If we dare to teach, we must be extremely careful of what it is we're teaching. He is not saying we shouldn't teach, but we will be judged more strictly on what we have taught. By teaching, we set ourselves up as having authority, which causes others to believe in what we say. Therefore, what a teacher says carries more weight with the listener. So if we teach the wrong things, we may cause others to go astray.

In verse 2 it says if we can keep from offending with our tongues, we will become complete and be able to control all parts of our lives. Our tongue is 'the weakest link'.

What is the purpose of a bit in a horse's mouth? What about a rudder on a ship? In the same way, a teacher is someone who guides others. What we say could cause someone to be guided in the wrong direction.

Verse 6 is a sharp image of how devastating sin can be. Our tongues can corrupt us entirely. We might live otherwise pure lives, but what we say can destroy, not only our testimony for Christ, but our souls by putting us in jeopardy of hell's fire. Even if we don't go to hell for the sins our tongues commit, we may cause others to turn away from Christ, causing them to go to hell.

Think of the forest as the lost souls around you. Think of your words as the spark that could send them all into the flames of hell.

Satan uses the tongue to divide people and pit them against each other. Hateful words are damaging because they spread destruction quickly, like a fire out of control. No one can stop the results once they are spoken. Even if we apologize later, the scars will remain, like charred wood that cannot be repaired.

Read James 3:7-8

Although we can tame all of earth's creatures, we can't tame our own tongues. If we could, we would be perfect and able to control all parts of our lives.

So, if no man can control his tongue, where is our hope? We are not fighting the tongue's fire on our own. The Holy Spirit will give us the power to monitor and control what we say if we ask. When we are offended, we need to turn to prayer so we can be reminded of God's love, and we won't react in a hateful manner. When we are criticized, we should turn to Christ to heal the hurt, rather than lash out.

Read James 3:9-12

Praise for God and ungodly speech should not be allowed to come out of the same mouth just as fresh water and salt water cannot come from the same spring. In the same way, we cannot produce both good and bad fruit. We may tell someone about Christ, but if we curse or gossip, that person is going to see us as hypocrites.

We shouldn't talk against another person because God made all of us in His image, and by making fun of someone else, or cursing them, we are committing a sin against God and His creation.

If you heard a tape recording of everything you said last week, how much would you want to edit out?

When you hear someone using foul language, how do you react? How does it make you feel about that person? How much can we learn about someone by the way they speak? What do others learn about you when they hear you speak?

Let's forget about foul language. In what other ways do we dishonor God with our tongues? Examples of an untamed tongue include gossiping, putting others down, bragging, manipulating, false teaching, exaggerating, complaining, flattering, bitterness, expressing anger, and lying.

Before you speak, ask yourself if what you are about to say is necessary, and is it kind?

Now James turns back to his main theme, which is the development of Christian behavior.

Read James 3:13-14

How do we show wisdom? By living a good life.

If we feel bitterness and envy or selfish ambition, or if we are quarrelsome with others, what should we do? Should we ignore these feelings and pretend they don't exist? Don't boast to others about these feelings because they are not something to be proud of. But don't lie about them either. You need to confess that you're having these feelings and try to rid yourself of them.

Read James 3:15-16

These feelings come from 'earthly wisdom', which is not from the Holy Spirit, but from Satan. If you have envy and selfishness in your life, it will cause disorder and sinfulness, making our lives confusing.

It's so easy for us to get drawn into the world's wisdom. We are constantly encouraged to "assert yourself", to "go for it", to "set high goals." We're constantly told we "deserve to do things for ourselves." This causes greed and destructive competitiveness. Seeking God's wisdom delivers us from the need to compare ourselves to others and to want what they have.

Many of us feel our lives spinning out of control sometimes. God wants us to be at peace and in control of our lives.

How many commandments are there? A total of 613 commandments are listed in the Law of Moses, most of which are in the book of Leviticus. Why did God make these rules? Was it to test our faith or to make our lives more difficult? Of course not. Throughout the scriptures, God doesn't give us rules to live by out of a need to control us. Each commandment He gives us is intended to make our lives easier, less confused, healthier, and more peaceful. The rules are our Father's way of guiding us through the chaos life throws at us.

Read James 3:17-18

I Corinthians 2:6-10 says *"We do, however, speak a message of wisdom among the mature, but not the wisdom of this age or of the rulers of this age, who are coming to nothing. No, we speak of God's secret wisdom, a wisdom that has been hidden and that God destined for our glory before time began. None of the rulers of this age understood it, for if they had, they would not have crucified the Lord of glory. However, as it is written: "No eye has seen, no ear has heard, no mind has conceived what God has prepared for those who love him"* (taken from Isaiah 64:4)—

"but God has revealed it to us by his Spirit. The Spirit searches all things, even the deep things of God."

This message of God's secret wisdom is revealed through the scripture that we are studying. It IS THE SECRET OF LIFE.

James has discussed two kinds of wisdom here. He speaks of worldly, unspiritual, demonic wisdom which produces such things as jealousy, selfish ambition, disharmony, and every foul practice. And the other is heavenly wisdom from above, from the Father.

Heavenly wisdom, wisdom which comes from the Holy Spirit's guidance, is virtuous, peace loving, considerate, humble, full of mercy and good fruit, impartial and genuine without hypocrisy.

The Holy Spirit reveals the truth to man, as said in verse 10 of 1 Corinthians 2 (above). Other scripture backs this up:

Read John 15:26

Read Romans 9:1

Read Ephesians 3:5

Read 1 Peter 1:12

Read 2 Peter 1:21

New Covenant truths are revealed to us through our relationship with the Holy Spirit. When Jesus ascended into Heaven, he left behind the Holy Spirit to guide us and remind us of His teachings.

Verse 18 warrants repeating: *"Peacemakers who sow in peace reap a harvest of righteousness."*

Matthew 5:9 says *"Blessed are the Peacemakers for they will be called Sons of God."*

If you live your life with these guidelines, you will be sowing the seeds of peace and 'reap a harvest of righteousness'.

What does the word righteousness mean to you? (Other words that describe righteousness are 'virtue', 'morality', 'decency', and 'honesty'). As Christians, righteousness is Jesus Christ, the righteous one, who alone makes us righteous. Righteousness comes through Him alone, not by our own attempts at virtuousness or goodness. Our lack of virtue, morality, decency, honesty, etc. is covered by the righteousness of Christ. His sacrifice on the cross, His death and resurrection is the righteousness of God that is now ours!

So James tells us a Christian will:
1. *live a good life*
2. *be humble in doing good deeds*
3. *will rid ourselves of bitter envy and selfish ambition*
4. *will be pure*
5. *will be peace-loving*
6. *will be considerate*
7. *will be submissive*
8. *will be full of mercy and good fruit*
9. *will be impartial and sincere*
10. *will harvest from our lives righteousness.*

God's Word to the wise:

Proverbs 10:5 -- The wise 'gathereth in summer' (does things in a timely manner)

Proverbs 11:12 -- The wise 'holdeth his peace' (doesn't berate others-keeps the peace)

Proverbs 12:15 -- The wise 'harkeneth unto counsel' (doesn't assume he's right all the time)

Proverbs 13:1 -- The wise 'heareth his Father's instruction' (follows parent's guidelines)

Proverbs 13:14 -- The wise 'depart from the snares of death' (a wise teacher can keep others from falling into the hands of Satan)

Proverbs 15:7 -- The wise 'disperse knowledge'

Proverbs 17:2 -- The wise 'shall have part of the inheritance among the brethren' (shall share in the riches of Heaven)

Proverbs 19:8 -- The wise 'loveth his own soul' (will take care of his soul's needs by living a good life and studying God's Word to achieve a better understanding from the Holy Spirit – feeding his soul)

Ecclesiastes 7:19 -- The wise 'are stronger than ten mighty men which are in the city' (through wisdom comes strength and power—by knowing how to live we gain power over ourselves and our destiny)

James – Chapter 4

Submitting to God's Will Rather Than Our Own

Read James 4:1-2

To covet is to desire to have what belongs to others. Many a war has been fought because of this. Conflicts and disputes among believers are always harmful. James explains these quarrels are a result of our evil desires battling within us – we want more possessions, more money, higher status, more recognition. When we want these things badly enough, we fight in order to obtain them. Coveting causes a battle between our desires and God's desires for us. Instead, we should submit ourselves to God, asking Him to help rid us of our selfishness and trust Him to provide our needs. Coveting causes a battle between our desires and God's desires for us.

Read James 4:3

Sometimes it seems God doesn't answer some prayers. Verse 3 tells us God DOES NOT answer all prayers. One reason for unanswered prayer is when the person praying is asking for the gratification of their own worldly pleasures. When we ask in selfishness, God does not answer selfish prayers. When we pray with wrong motives, we misuse the gift of prayer, raising false hopes, treating prayer as a magic charm.

If you could ask God for anything, what would it be? Would He answer this one for you?

We can't know if He will answer it or not. Jesus taught us to pray "Thy will be done." God is sovereign. Prayer helps us to align our desires with God's desires, to prioritize our lives according to His will.

So is James saying in verse 3 we shouldn't want to enjoy life? Of course not! But these pleasures cannot be placed above God or other people. Pleasure that keeps us from pleasing God is sinful. When we seek pleasure at the expense of others' or at the expense of obeying God, that's when our pleasures become sinful.

Read James 4:4-6

Adulterous people? God is calling people who love the world 'spiritual adulterers' because they cannot love both God and the world. This is the same as cheating on your spouse.

Verse 5 seems to confuse even the greatest theologians. The same Greek word, pneu'ma, is used to mean "spirit of God", "human spirit", "evil spirit", and "Jesus's own spirit." So it is difficult to interpret exactly which meaning is referred to here. Some believe the word 'spirit' here is referring to the spirit of mankind that causes us to have fleshly desires. (Sin has its origin in man's flesh.) Others believe it is referring to the Holy Spirit of God, which feels jealousy when other things are placed above Him in our hearts and minds.

In verse 6, James is quoting Proverbs 3:34. God will only be able to help us if we humble ourselves. Sin is forgiven by the grace of our Lord, but pride will stand in the way of God's grace. God opposes the proud and He is always available with grace when we need it.

Read James 4:7-10

Through the Holy Spirit, we have the power to resist Satan and make him flee from us. As Christians, we have three enemies we must guard against: the flesh, the world, and Satan.

These passages suggest the need of unceasing self-examination. We need to constantly draw nigh to God, cleanse our hands, purify our hearts and to humble ourselves. Submission and humility are the secret to obtaining God's grace.

"Come near to God and He will come near to you." I love this verse because it assures me God will not turn away from me when I reach out to Him.

"Double-Minded": This is an expansion of Jesus's statement in Matthew 6:24, that a person cannot serve God and worldly things. This is also similar to John's warning against love of the world in I John 2:15-17.

Read Matthew 6:24

Read 1 John 2:15-17

Sin means we have offended God and merit His judgment. Sin must be treated with due abhorrence.

Is James telling us it is wrong to laugh and be joyful? No, he is saying if we are sinners or trying to live a double life (partially as Christians and partially enjoying worldly things), we should repent and humble ourselves. This is how we receive the grace of God. When he says 'grieve, mourn and wail, he means for us to be sorrowful for sins and be repentant, not simply say 'oops, I'm sorry' and continue on our way.

James has given us five ways we can come near to God:

1. Submit to God (vs. 4:7): Yield to His authority and will, and commit your life to Him and His control.
2. Resist the devil (vs. 4:7): Don't allow Satan to entice and tempt you.
3. Wash your hands and purify your hearts (vs. 4:8): Lead a pure life. Be cleansed from sin. Replace your desire to sin with your desire to experience God's purity.
4. Grieve and mourn and wail (vs. 4:9): Be sincerely sorrowful for your sins. Don't be afraid to express deep heartfelt sorrow for what you have done.
5. Humble yourself before the Lord (vs. 4:10) and He will lift you up: Recognize the fact that your worth comes from God alone. Despite our human shortcomings, God reaches out to us in love and gives us worth and dignity.

Read James 4:11-12

Back to using the tongue, but this time he is pointing out how absurd it is for us to set ourselves up as judge of another sinner.

How is speaking against another person also speaking against 'the law'?

The 'royal law' is "loving one another." When you criticize someone, you are not showing love toward that person. Try to always say things which are beneficial to others and this will help cure you of finding fault, increasing your ability to obey God's law.

James is telling us there is only one law-giver and one judge. By judging others, we are trying to put ourselves in God's place, or in essence, playing God.

Read James 4:13-17

God has a definite plan for each of His people, but we have 'free will' and have the choice to choose our way or His. When we pray, or when we make plans for our future, we should always be asking for His will to be done in our lives.

Your future is in God's hands, so don't be making plans for the future without considering they might change. When you make plans, leave room for change, because God may have other plans for you. If you put God's desires at the center of your plans, He won't disappoint you.

Don't be deceived into thinking you have lots of time remaining to live for Christ, to enjoy your loved ones, or to do what you know you should. Live for God today, then no matter when your life ends, you will have fulfilled God's plan for your life.

If you know you should do something good, but you don't do it, you are sinning.

We all know if we do something we shouldn't do, we are sinning. But here is a new slant on it. If you neglect to do what is right, that is also a sin. It's a sin to speak evil of someone; but it is also a sin to avoid someone when you know he or she needs your friendship. So we need to be more diligent in helping others. Always be willing to help as the Holy Spirit guides you.

Consider this: If you knew you only had 3 months to live, what are some things you would want to do? What would become most important in your life? Are those things, which are most important to you, also what is most important to God for your life? Will you proceed with your will, or bend to God's will?

James – Chapter 5

Read James 5:1-6

There must have been a lot of rich men in the Judean Church who were consumed with worldly pleasures. This is the fourth time in this short letter James blasts the rich.

Here, he writes about the worthlessness of riches. It's not a sin to have money. Money is necessary to live in this world. But money will be worthless when Christ returns, so we need to be storing up the kind of treasures that will be worthwhile in heaven. So money is not the problem. Christians need it to live and support their families, churches need it to do their work effectively, and missionaries need it to spread the gospel.

1 Timothy 6:10 says *"For the love of money is a root of all kinds of evil. Some people, eager for money, have wandered from the faith and pierced themselves with many griefs."*

Somehow this has been translated as 'money' being the root of all evil. But it's the LOVE of money that causes the problem, making people so greedy they are willing to cheat others in order to obtain more.

Read Matthew 6:19-21

Here's a thought: Although this is not what the verse above is saying, I want you to think about this idea. You reveal where your heart is, where your loyalties are, by how you handle and spend your money. Look through your checkbook, or take note of how you spend your money. If someone was watching you, would they be able to tell your loyalties are to God? Or would they see selfish self-indulgence of worldly pleasures instead?

In vs. 5, James is comparing the rich self-indulgent people to cattle that continue to eat and fatten themselves up on the day they are to be slaughtered, totally unaware of their coming destruction.

In vs. 6, he writes about how hoarding money and exploiting employees causes us to be murderous. The 'innocent men' he speaks of here are defenseless people, laborers, poor people who could not pay their debts. Back in the first century, whenever a person couldn't pay his debts, he was thrown into prison or forced to sell all of his possessions. Sometimes people were even forced to sell their family members into slavery. They often died of starvation. So in point of fact, the rich man who would not pay his laborers was guilty of murdering them because of his own self-indulgence and greed.

Read James 5:7-8

One day the Lord will return and all of our suffering will be over. Keep your eyes and your heart fixed on that day.

When a farmer plants his crops, he must be patient while waiting for his crops to grow. But the farmer doesn't just sit around and wait. He has a lot of work to do to ensure he has a good harvest. His entire summer is full of laboring until the harvest. In the same way, we must be patient in awaiting the return of Christ, and we must stay busy doing the work God has commissioned us to do—teaching the gospel to all the ends of the earth.

We cannot make Christ return any faster, just as the farmer cannot make his crops come in any faster. But both the farmer and the Christian must live by faith, looking toward the future reward for their labors. Don't live as if Jesus will never come back; continue to work faithfully for Him.

Read James 5:9

Read Matthew 7:1-5

We can't be shifting blame to others when things aren't getting done. Keep your focus on what you should be doing and not what others are NOT doing. Sometimes it's easier to blame others rather than owning up to our share of the responsibility. Before you judge others for their shortcomings, remember Christ is the judge and will come to evaluate each of us.

Read Matthew 25:31-46

So Christ will come and He will judge each of us according to the things we have done, or not done. In Jesus's own words, when we cause pain to another human being, we cause Him pain, or when we do something to help someone else, we are helping Him.

Read James 5:10-11

Be patient. God will come through. James reminds us of how patient the prophets had to be. He goes on to mention Job who persevered through many trials and tribulations. He and the prophets were faithful, knowing they were doing the work God wanted them to do. And God eventually rewarded them for their perseverance and faithfulness.

F.A.C.T.S.

Read James 5:12

Why do we find it necessary to swear to something? It's because we want people to believe what we're saying is the truth. But if we earn the reputation of being an honest person, we wouldn't have to swear. People would believe us just on our word alone.

If you're prone to exaggeration or lying, people will doubt your word. By avoiding lies, half-truths, and omissions of the truth, you will become known as a trustworthy person and people will believe your simple yes or no.

James is not condemning the taking of solemn oaths. He is condemning the flippant use of God's name or a sacred object to guarantee the truth of what is spoken.

Read James 5:13-16

Here James is telling his readers how we should handle our problems.

- If we are in trouble, we should pray. Hand your troubles over to God and **believe** He will help you through whatever it is.
- Unhappy? Sing songs of praise. This will inevitably lift your spirits. When we sing songs of praise, we are reminded of God's love and mercy, which helps us put our trivial problems into perspective.
- If we are sick, we should contact the leaders of the church so they can pray for us. He mentions oil because in scripture, oil was both a medicine and a symbol of the Spirit of God. Either way, Jesus is Lord over both the body and the spirit. So whether we are 'sick' in spirit or physically sick, the members of Christ's body (the church) should be able to count on the other members for support and prayer. Elders and church members

should stay alert to pray for the needs of all the church's members.

Notice in verse 15, it isn't the oil that heals, but the "prayer of faith." The Lord heals when he hears our prayers "offered in faith." All prayers are subject to God's will and His time-table. So again, we must be patient and faithful.

On the network news a while back, it was reported that doctors and scientists have now come to the conclusion prayer helps people get well. Of course, some of them are trying to say it's only because we 'think ourselves well', but others are convinced there is more to it than that. Isn't it refreshing when the rest of the world figures out what we've known all along?

James goes on to write about spiritual healing. If someone has sinned, we are to pray for them so they may be forgiven and healed. The sinner must repent, but by going to the Church and having others pray for them, other things are accomplished.

First, if someone has sinned against another individual, he or she must ask their forgiveness. By praying together, this encourages both to forgive and put the problem behind them.

Second, if the sin has somehow affected the church, we need to confess it publicly so the problems can be set right.

Third, sometimes we need loving support as we struggle with a sin. By confessing it to others and having them help us through it, it helps us conquer the temptation.

The practice of confessing publicly has at times been abused by churches and pastors or elders, bringing more damage to the individual and to the church, sometimes breaking the relationship between the one being forced to confess and God. The goal is to give support and love to the individual, not admonish or embarrass him/her. Public confession should be a person's choice, not forced upon them.

In today's society, there are all kinds of excuses made for every committed act. We all need to own responsibility for sins rather than making excuses for them by giving them a psychological name or neuroses.

God already knows what our sins are, so why do we need to confess to Him? Verbalizing and repenting of our sins helps us own our thoughts and behaviors. Confessing and having a genuine sorrow that causes us to actually stop committing the sin gives us healing so our prayers may be heard by the Almighty. He knows our hearts. He knows if we are sincere.

Read James 5:17-18

Sometimes we tend to use prayer as a last resort, when all else has failed. But this is backwards—prayer should come first. The Christian's most powerful resource is communion with God through prayer. The more we use this resource, the stronger we will become.

James talks about how Elijah's prayers were answered. During his struggle against King Ahab and idolatry, Elijah once prayed for a drought that would cripple the evil king. God responded by withholding rain from the land for over three years. Later, Elijah prayed for rain, and it came in torrents.

James comments on the faith of Elijah by saying he was only a man, like us. In other words, our prayers have the same potential power as the prayers of Elijah, since he was just as human as we are.

But as James has stressed all the way through his letter, prayers of such effectiveness are possible only when we pray in faith and pray with the proper motives. Prayer is the conduit for taking any and every concern to God—seeking his aid and expressing our thanks to Him for His blessings.

Read James 5:19-20

When one of our fellow Christians falls away, we should try to help them get back on track. By taking the initiative, praying for them, and acting in love we might be able to bring them back to God and his forgiveness. By doing this, you will have saved this person from the fires of hell. This is the kind of behavior for which we will receive rewards on judgment day.

This letter by James stresses faith in action. Living right is evidence of faith. Members of the Church must serve with compassion, speak lovingly and truthfully, live in obedience to God's commandments, and love each other. We must be an example of heaven on earth, drawing people to Christ through our love for God and for each other. If we truly believe God's Word, we will live it day by day.

God's Word is not just something we read and think about, but something we do.

The Letters to the

THESSALONIANS

Paul Of Tarsus

While James was teaching the Jews and writing his letter to the 12 tribes of Israel and becoming the chairman of the Council of the Church in Jerusalem, Paul was busy teaching the Gentiles.

Paul was born around 10 AD in Tarsus, a city in Cilicia, which is now a part of Turkey. He was considered a Jew because his parents were Jewish. Yet he was born in Tarsus, which gave him Roman citizenship. So he was a Roman citizen with a Greek culture and Jewish faith.

He learned to speak and think like a Greek, but remained loyal to his Jewish heritage. At the age of 18, he was sent to Jerusalem to be educated as a rabbi and, therefore, learned the Old Testament thoroughly. Being the devoted Jew, he refused to believe Jesus was the Messiah and became a persecutor of those Jews who did believe. As such, he was commissioned by the high priest to travel north and arrest any followers of Jesus.

While traveling north on the road to Damascus, the risen Jesus appeared to him, and Paul was converted to Christianity by this encounter. He was also left blind from looking upon the Lord. He knew it wasn't a dream because, not only was he blinded, but his troops also heard the loud voice of Jesus, although they didn't see Him or understand His words.

At about 26 years old (36 AD), right after his conversion, Paul went to Arabia, which is now Jordan, and then returned to Damascus. He preached there for three years and then traveled to Jerusalem, then to Tarsus, Syria, and Cilicia. This took another 4 years.

At the approximate age of 36, Paul took his first missionary journey, covering about 1400 miles, with Barnabas and Mark (also known as John-Mark who wrote the Gospel of Mark). He moved quickly from place to place as he angered the Jews with his bold and controversial speeches.

In 2 Corinthians 11:24-28, we learn from his own words what his life was like during this time.

"Five times I received from the Jews the forty lashes minus one. Three times I was beaten with rods, once I was pelted with stones, three times I was shipwrecked, I spent a night and a day in the open sea, I have been constantly on the move. I have been in danger from rivers, in danger from bandits, in danger from my fellow Jews, in danger from Gentiles; in danger in the city, in danger in the country, in danger at sea; and in danger from false believers. I have labored and toiled and have often gone without sleep; I have known hunger and thirst and have often gone without food; I have been cold and naked. Besides everything else, I face daily the pressure of my concern for all the churches."

Now we are up to about 48 AD, about the time James wrote the book of James.

At about age 40, Paul began his second missionary journey, covering roughly 2800 miles, accompanied by Silas and later joined by young Timothy. On this trip he traveled to northwest Asia Minor and crossed to Macedonia, bringing Christianity to Europe for the first time.

It was approximately 51 AD when they visited Thessalonica, the capital of Macedonia. They preached there until they were forced to flee to Berea. Although they were only in Thessalonica for a short period of time, they were able to establish a church with a group of devoted Christians. From Berea, Paul fled to Athens, leaving Timothy and Silas behind.

Later, after joining Paul in Athens, Timothy was sent back to Thessalonica to help lead the newly formed church. Paul, failing to convince the people in Athens of the Messiahship of Jesus, moved on to Corinth, where he stayed for 18 months working as a tentmaker and teaching about Christ, which resulted in a large church being formed in Corinth.

Still anxious about the immature congregation he had left behind in Thessalonica, he received a report from Timothy in about 52 AD and wrote the two letters of encouragement and instruction known as 1 & 2 Thessalonians.

F.A.C.T.S.

Paul, as painted by Bartolomeo Montagna
(As shown on the Wikipedia website)

1 Thessalonians – Chapter 1

In the simplest terms, Paul's letter in 1 Thessalonians is about pleasing God. Although the Thessalonians were already doing so, Paul wanted to encourage them to do even more. Paul seems to have a loving and gentle manner in his writing. You can tell he truly cares for his fellow Christians.

Read 1 Thessalonians 1:1-3

Paul remembers the Thessalonians as very faithful and loving, with a strong hope in the Lord Jesus Christ. The faith Paul is talking about here produces action. Many Christians use faith as an excuse to do nothing because "God will take care of everything." Faith should prompt us into action, not make us complacent. The hope Paul speaks of here is not unfounded wishful thinking, but a firm confidence in Jesus Christ and His return.

Read 1 Thessalonians 1:4

The Greek word for brothers and sisters (adelphoi) refers here to believers, both men and women, as part of God's family.

The first thing Paul wants these young Christians to know about is not the mechanics of the Christian life, but the fact God is at work in their lives now since they have come to believe. He lets them know God loves them and has chosen them.

Read 1 Thessalonians 1:5

Paul refers to the 'good news' as "our gospel." Although this 'gospel' he has taught is not clearly spelled out in the letter, we can figure it out from what he does say. The 'power' he speaks of here could mean a couple of things; (1) the power of the Holy Spirit which leads them, or (2) the power of the Gospel itself which brings salvation, freeing them from the bondage of sin.

Read 1 Thessalonians 1:6

Paul commends them for 'imitating' him, and in doing so they are imitating Christ. He once again is letting them know God is at work in their lives through His word. Paul says in spite of their suffering, they stood firm in the Lord and were joyful in their faith. This gives us some insight about how they must have been rebuked for their beliefs.

Read 1 Thessalonians 1:7

Macedonia and Achaia were the 2 provinces into which Greece was divided. Thessalonica was on the important Egnatian Way, and was a busy seaport and the capital city of Macedonia.

Read 1 Thessalonians 1:8-9

These people had joyfully told everyone of their 'good news' about Christ. Because of how they had changed, their story had spread throughout all the land.

Everywhere Paul went, he heard the great stories of the Thessalonian church and its faith and works. Paul is letting them know how proud he is of them for their faithfulness and the example they have become to those around them. The Gospel has spread because of their exemplary representation of Christ. This is a suburb statement of how everyone should respond to the Gospel.

Read 1 Thessalonians 1:10

Paul also wants them to know Christ is coming back, and Jesus's return is an inspiration for young Christians. This hope and promise should keep them strong in their faith and keep them looking forward to that day and living their lives for that event. This same hope and promise is ours today, and should keep us strong in our faith and looking forward to that event, and living our lives in preparation for that day.

1 Thessalonians – Chapter 2

If you were accused of a crime you did not commit, how would you respond? This is what happened to Paul, and this letter is his response.

Read 1 Thessalonians 2:1-2

Paul tells the Thessalonian church his teaching them was not in vain. Although Paul, Silas, and Timothy had been treated harshly and suffered for spreading the gospel, they had done it anyway and were glad they had persevered.

Read 1 Thessalonians 2:3-4

Their teachings had not been for any wrong reasons. There were no selfish alternative motives as their accusers claimed. But they had done what God had entrusted them to do.

Read 1 Thessalonians 2:5-8

In their teaching, they never used flattery to win anyone over or asked for anything from their listeners. Neither did they do anything to glorify themselves—even though, as

Christ's apostles, they would have had every right to ask for assistance with the creature comforts. But they never asked for more than the basic necessities, and were gentle and loving and treated their listeners as sick children. And they did this because they loved them and had not only taught them the gospel, but devoted their hearts and souls to them.

Read 1 Thessalonians 2:9

They worked for their keep rather than be a burden on anyone as they taught the gospel.

Read 1 Thessalonians 2:10-12

Paul asked that they remember how well they had behaved – holy and just—how they had comforted them and taken care of them the way a father cares for his children, so they could become children of God.

From the way this reads, it is obvious the enemies of the Christians were attacking Paul's character, trying to make him look like an opportunist who was trying to take these people for a ride (a con-artist). Paul is writing here to defend himself. He reminds them he never asked anything of them or took anything from them. He also reminds them he had done nothing but love them and he had been unselfish in his preaching and had lived as an example to them as a good Christian.

Read 1 Thessalonians 2:13

Paul is thankful these people accepted what he had preached as coming from God, and therefore they had been transformed by God.

Read 1 Thessalonians 2:14-16

The Thessalonians to whom this letter was written had become followers of the Church of God in Jesus Christ, and because of their devotion they had suffered from persecution from both Gentiles and Jews.

Jews had killed Jesus and their own prophets and had persecuted Paul and his fellow Christians, and God was not pleased by their actions. These Jews were not good for mankind because they were forbidding the teaching of salvation. Therefore, Paul says, they will suffer God's wrath.

Verses 15-16 indicates the Jews had chased Paul out of Thessalonica and were still relentlessly venting their wrath against the rest of the Christians Paul had left behind in the newly established church. Paul tries to comfort them by explaining that all Christians, and even Christ Himself, had suffered for their beliefs and this suffering was to be expected. He also tells them there is no hope of repentance for those who do the persecuting and no escape for their doom on the Day of Judgment.

Read 1 Thessalonians 2:17-18

Although Paul, Silas, and Timothy could not be with the Thessalonians in person, their hearts were with them and they desired to see them soon. They would have been back with them, but Satan prevented it. Paul had tried twice to return to them, only to be stopped by Satan.

Acts 16:6-7 tells us more about this time period and what was happening with Paul: *"Paul and his companions traveled throughout the region of Phrygia and Galatia, having been kept by the Holy Spirit from preaching the word in the province of Asia. 7 When they came to the border of Mysia, they tried to enter Bithynia, but the Spirit of Jesus would not allow them to."*

We learn from these verses that Paul was kept from going to certain places by the Holy Spirit, but in his letter to the Thessalonians he says he was hindered by Satan. How he knew when it was the Holy Spirit hindering him and when it was Satan, arch-enemy of the church, is an unanswered question we can only guess about, but Paul knew the difference.

Read 1 Thessalonians 2:19-20

Once again Paul ends the chapter with a mention of Christ's eventual return. He tells the Thessalonian Christians they were the reason for his and Silas's and Timothy's joy and they made all their suffering worthwhile. Then he expresses that on the day of Christ's return when He gives Paul his rewards, his brightest star (or his best accomplishment) will be the Thessalonian Church ("his hope, joy, crown & glory") because so many souls had been won for Christ.

We judge the success or failure of our work with other people by how they respond. There are certain standards of behavior Christians should follow as they try to reach out to people. They should be unselfish and caring of the other person's soul and their needs.

Paul was an example to the Thessalonians in showing them how to be a Christian:

- He was courageous and steadfast – no matter how much persecution he faced, he continued to do God's will; (verse 1-2)
- He was gentle and affectionate – he loved his fellow Christians and tried to encourage them by treating them as a father did his child; (verse 5-8)
- He was full of integrity – he worked for his own keep and never asked anything from anyone; (verse 9)
- He was an example – by the way he lived and treated other people; (verse 10-12)
- He was eager to please God rather than man. (verse 3-4)

1 Thessalonians – Chapter 3

According to Acts 17:14-15, Paul had gone to Athens alone and then sent for Silas and Timothy to join him from Berea.

The believers immediately sent Paul to the coast, but Silas and Timothy stayed at Berea. Those who escorted Paul brought him to Athens and then left with instructions for Silas and Timothy to join him as soon as possible.

In chapter 3 of 1 Thessalonians, Paul continues to tell the Thessalonians of his longing to be with them. He was concerned about the new-born Thessalonian Church and had sent Timothy back to encourage them under the bitter persecution they were undergoing.

Read 1 Thessalonians 3:1

Although Paul wanted more than anything to return to Thessalonica himself to be with the new church members, he didn't feel it was safe, so he sent Timothy instead.

Read 1 Thessalonians 3:2-3

"Co-worker in God's service" or "God's fellow worker": This is an interesting way of viewing Christian service. Timothy was sent back to help encourage them in their Christian service and help make them stronger in their faith.

Paul says Christians are to expect troubles. It is our destiny to have to face them. These trials are not disasters because they advance God's purposes.

Read 1 Thessalonians 3:4

Paul says when they were with them they had warned them they would be persecuted, and it happened just as he had said.

Read 1 Thessalonians 3:5

Paul's major concern over the new believers in Thessalonica was "the tempter" would discourage them and cause their work there to be wasted.

The 'tempter,' of course, is Satan. Some churches today are afraid to preach about Satan. Some people, although they believe in God and Heaven, refuse to believe Satan exists or that there is a hell. Yet he is spoken of in every major division of the New Testament. He is supreme among evil spirits as we see in John 16:8-11…

When he comes, he will prove the world to be in the wrong about sin and righteousness and judgment: about sin, because people do not believe in me; about righteousness, because I am going to the Father, where you can see me no longer; and about judgment, because the prince of this world now stands condemned.

…& Ephesians 2:1-2

As for you, you were dead in your transgressions and sins, in which you used to live when you followed the ways of this world and of the ruler of the kingdom of the air, the spirit who is now at work in those who are disobedient.

Satan's activities can affect us physically and the spiritually as we read in the following scriptures:

2 Corinthians 12:7 *"… or because of these surpassingly great revelations. Therefore, in order to keep me from becoming conceited, I was given a thorn in my flesh, a messenger of Satan, to torment me."*

Matthew 13:38-39 *"The field is the world, and the good seed stands for the people of the kingdom. The weeds are the people of the evil one, and the enemy who sows them is the devil. The harvest is the end of the age, and the harvesters are angels."*

Mark 4:15 *"Some people are like seed along the path, where the word is sown. As soon as they hear it, Satan comes and takes away the word that was sown in them."*

2 Corinthians 4:4 *"The god of this age has blinded the minds of unbelievers, so that they cannot see the light of the gospel that displays the glory of Christ, who is the image of God."*

Satan tempted Jesus and continues to tempt Jesus' servants as we read in the following verses:

Luke 22:3 *"Then Satan entered Judas, called Iscariot, one of the Twelve."*

1 Corinthians 7:5 *"Do not deprive each other except perhaps by mutual consent and for a time, so that you may devote yourselves to prayer. Then come together again so that Satan will not tempt you because of your lack of self-control."*

But Satan has already been defeated…

Colossians 2:15 *"And having disarmed the powers and authorities, he (Jesus) made a public spectacle of them, triumphing over them by the cross."*

Christians need to be on their guard and not be overwhelmed by him.

Ephesians 6:16 *"In addition to all this, take up the shield of faith, with which you can extinguish all the flaming arrows of the evil one."*

Satan's final overthrow is certain:

Revelation 20:10 *"And the devil, who deceived them, was thrown into the lake of burning sulfur, where the beast and the false prophet had been thrown. They will be tormented day and night for ever and ever."*

Now let's get back to 1 Thessalonians:

Read 1 Thessalonians 3:6

Timothy returned with the news of their steadfastness and devotion and Paul is filled with joy over this news.

This is the only time the Greek term meaning 'good news' is used by Paul for something other than the gospel.

There were three things Timothy reported about the Thessalonians which made Paul happy:
- Their faith (right attitude toward God),
- Their love (right attitude toward man),
- Their good memories of Paul and desire to see him again (right attitude toward Paul).

Read 1 Thessalonians 3:7

Although Paul is in trouble and is suffering, he explains to them he is joyful because their faith has encouraged him.

Read 1 Thessalonians 3:8

Because the Thessalonians have so much faith and are steadfast, this makes Paul's heart soar with happiness, making him feel alive with purpose. That's what he meant by "for now we really live."

Read 1 Thessalonians 3:9

Paul could have congratulated himself on a job well-done because it was his evangelism that had been effective in Thessalonica, but instead he thanked God for the joy he had from what God had done there.

Read 1 Thessalonians 3:10

"Night and Day" doesn't mean there were two set times he prayed, but he means "frequent and constant prayer." The Greek word which is translated as 'most earnestly' is a strong and unusual compound word that expresses immense passion.

Paul's prayer for the Thessalonians was that they would soon be with them and be able to supply what is needed to keep them strong in their faith.

These new Christians needed moral teaching and disciplinary training. They also needed doctrinal guidance such as clearing up any confusion about Christ's return.

Their faith is obviously uppermost in Paul's mind because this is the fifth time in this chapter he mentions their faith.

Read 1 Thessalonians 3:11

Paul frequently breaks into prayer in the middle of his letters. This is an example. It shows how much he wishes to return to them.

Read 1 Thessalonians 3:12

He prays for them to remain strong and love each other just as he loves them.

Read 1 Thessalonians 3:13

Again, Paul reminds them of Christ's eventual return. He says we should prepare for this event by setting ourselves apart for God. "Holy ones" is a term used of the Christians (or saints) in many New Testament passages.

Ask yourself these questions:

What personal accomplishments will count for something when we stand in the presence of Christ?

What practical things can we do to help strengthen and encourage others in their faith?

How does Satan hinder or stop our efforts or plans?

How do we resist the temptations that hinder our spiritual progress?

In what ways can we prepare this week to get ready for Christ's return?

1 Thessalonians – Chapter 4

Think about the people you come in contact with each day and how they view sex. How much of this attitude do you think is influenced by the media? Immorality is still something each of us has to deal with on a daily basis. Humans haven't changed in all of the years between when this letter was written and today.

Read 1 Thessalonians 4:1-2

When he had been there and set up the church, Paul had obviously instructed them on how they should live. The word Paul used for "live" was the Greek word for 'walk'. Paul often uses this metaphor when speaking of the Christian way. But now he wanted them to strive harder to live right in Jesus' name. Paul was not being arrogant here, but speaking with the authority from Jesus Christ.

1 Corinthians 2:16 tells us *"for, who has known the mind of the Lord so as to instruct him? But we have the mind of Christ."*

Paul says through the Lord Jesus' he has the authority to give these instructions.

Read 1 Thessalonians 4:3-8

'Sanctification' is used here to mean sexual purity. Paul would not compromise God's clear and demanding standards.

Immorality was very common among the heathen people and chastity was considered an unreasonable restriction, just as it is in today's society. It's possible in Timothy's report he had mentioned some cases of moral laxness among the Christians causing Paul to respond with these thoughts in his letter.

We need to have self-control. The Greek words used here seemed to indicate he was speaking of them obtaining their own wife so they would not be lusting after other men's wives.

The basic idea of this letter is for Christians to set ourselves apart for God and His return by setting ourselves apart from the ungodly by being morally pure. Christians are SUPPOSED TO BE DIFFERENT!!

The Greek word for brother or sister (adelphos) refers here to a believer, whether man or woman, as part of God's family.

'Wrong his brother' means to invade the rights of another's home. Sexual sin harms others. Paul seems to be speaking of adultery here or lusting after other men's wives. Adultery causes harm or pain to the spouse; premarital sex wrongs the future spouse. By saying the 'Lord will punish', Paul is giving them a motive to be chaste.

As Christians, we are to keep ourselves as pure as humanly possible and live holy lives, not only in our sexual conduct, but in all aspects of our lives. If we do not do this, we are rejecting God, for he gives us the Holy Spirit which cannot exist where there is sin. So by not living a holy life, we push the Holy Spirit out of our lives, rejecting Him.

Read 1 Thessalonians 4:9-10

Here Paul speaks of "brotherly love", or love between believers, men and women. Greek word used here was 'philadelphia' which specifically means love between the children of the same Father, male and female. In the Bible, this word is always used to mean love of fellow believers in Christ.

In Acts 17:4, it says *"Some of the Jews were persuaded and joined Paul and Silas, as did a large number of God-fearing Greeks and quite a few prominent women."*

From this verse, we know there were also women among the believers.

It seems there were quite a few within the church who had plenty of money, and they had taken the Christian doctrine of charity very seriously and were dispersing what they could to the poorer brethren of ALL the Macedonian churches. They were becoming very well known for their charity. Paul commends them for this.

Read 1 Thessalonians 4:11-12

But at the same time, their charity had given those who received the money an opportunity to be lazy and not work, so Paul rebukes their laziness. They had the mindset that 'God would provide' until His return. How often do Christians today fall into this inaccurate belief? Being willing to live off your neighbors was contrary to every principle of brotherly love. Able-bodied beggars enjoyed others brotherly love while they themselves practiced the very essence of self-love. This type of life could not win the respect of non-Christians. But if the non-Christians saw them working hard and leading a quiet and moral life, this would be a better witness to them of how God intends His people to live. This reminds me of the Quakers and the Amish people. We look at those people and, whether we agree with their beliefs or not, we can't help but respect them. They are a perfect example of what Paul is speaking of here.

Christians should strive to live a quiet life, mind their own business, and work to support themselves in order to earn the respect of non-Christians.

Is it possible to be a good Christian while being sexually immoral? A good person who loves other people maybe, but not a good Christian. These two things seem to get confused in today's society.

Paul changes his focus from his concerns about how they are living to their concerns about their loved ones who had passed away.

Read 1 Thessalonians 4:13-18

This is the main topic of the entire letter, the Second Coming. It's mentioned in every chapter, which implies Paul must have given it particular emphasis in his preaching in Thessalonica. The Second Coming is referred to in almost every New Testament book, but the chapters that explain it most fully are Matthew 24, 25, Luke 21, 1 Thessalonians 4, 5, and 2 Peter 3.

1 Thessalonians is the first or second of the written books of the Bible, and speaks of the Lord coming again. The last of the New Testament books is Revelation, of which the final message is "I come quickly." So the New Testament, when speaking chronologically, begins and ends with this message.

"Fallen asleep" is a Scriptural expression for the Christian's death. The Greek word used, as Jesus taught it, did not mean to lapse into a state of unconsciousness until the day of resurrection. It means an intermediate state of conscious bliss.

The Thessalonians were concerned for their loved ones who had already passed away before the Second Coming. These people believed Christ would come back in their lifetime. They honestly thought 'everlasting life' meant

Christians would not die. They didn't understand the Second Coming could be thousands of years in the future. Yet some of their fellow Christians had passed away and this confused them. They were worried they might miss the event of the return of Christ if they were to die before it happened. So Paul is trying to set their minds at ease.

Also, in verse 13, Paul is reminding them of the assurance we have of life after death which non-believers don't have, leaving them with no hope. Notice Paul did not say Christ 'fell asleep'. Christ bore the full horror of death and conquered it!

Verse 15 indicates Christ had given this instruction while He was here.

The Lord's return follows a certain sequence of events. "The Lord himself will come down from heaven with a loud command, with the voice of the archangel, and with the trumpet call of God."

This is similar to Jesus' words in Matthew 24:30-31:

"Then will appear the sign of the Son of Man in heaven. And then all the peoples of the earth will mourn when they see the Son of Man coming on the clouds of heaven, with power and great glory. And he will send his angels with a loud trumpet call, and they will gather his elect from the four winds, from one end of the heavens to the other.. The dead in Christ shall rise first."

Archangel: the only archangel mentioned in the Bible is Michael.

Jude 9 *"But even the archangel Michael, when he was disputing with the devil about the body of Moses, did not himself dare to condemn him for slander but said, "The Lord rebuke you!""*

Daniel 10:13 *"But the prince of the Persian kingdom resisted me twenty-one days. Then Michael, one of the chief princes, came to help me, because I was detained there with the king of Persia."*

Compare Acts 1:9 *"After he said this, he was taken up before their very eyes, and a cloud hid him from their sight."*

& Rev. 1:7 *"Look, he is coming with the clouds, and every eye will see him, even those who pierced him; and all peoples on earth will mourn because of him." So shall it be! Amen."*

Jesus went away in the "clouds", and so He will return. "The clouds" will be his triumphal chariot. The angels will be with Him, in all the glory of heaven, as we are told in Matthew 25:31: *"When the Son of Man comes in his glory, and all the angels with him, he will sit on his glorious throne."*

The saints of past ages will be raised, those still in the flesh will be changed, and the whole Church will rise in joyful welcome to the Returning Savior, to be with Him forevermore.

In verse 17, the words "caught up" is the only CLEAR reference to what has been referred to as the Rapture. The word "rapture" is never used in the Bible. "Rapture", in the context of the end days, is an English noun derived from the Latin verb rapiō, meaning "caught up" or "taken away." The word "Rapture" is interchangeable with the words "caught up." It all means the same thing, so the Rapture is supported by scripture even though that word is not used. More will be studied about this topic in studies of other books of the Bible that delve into it more thoroughly.

In verse 18, we are told to encourage each other by reminding each other of our eventual triumph. It thrills us through and through to think of it. We need to remind each other of the time when we will be with the Lord forever, to encourage each other in our faith. This last sentence is meant as a comfort for bereaved Christians who have lost a loved one. We know we will see them again when Christ returns.

F.A.C.T.S.

I lost my father on March 19, 2011. Although I grieve, the knowledge he is with our Lord and Savior has sustained me. I picture my dad's smile and how excited he must be to be with Jesus and the saints who went before him—and it makes me smile. I rejoice that one day I will join him on those golden streets.

1 Thessalonians – Chapter 5

Read 1 Thessalonians 5:1

"times and dates" – There have always been Christians who tried to fix the time and date of Christ's return, but apparently the Thessalonians were not among them. They understood Paul's teachings that no man would know the time of Christ's return.

Read 1 Thessalonians 5:2

"The day of the Lord" is the climax of all things—also known as the day of redemption.

"Like a thief in the night" means, although there will be some signs, the coming will be as unexpected as a thief in the night.

Read 1 Thessalonians 5:3

"destruction" does not mean annihilation here, but exclusion from the Lord's presence, thus the ruin of life and all its accomplishments.

"suddenly" is used to stress the surprise of unbelievers.
"labor pains" is a great analogy.

Although a woman knows approximately when her child is due and that the event is inevitable, she is always taken by surprise when the labor pains actually begin. Also, there is no escape for her. She cannot run away from the pain. Today we could take this analogy a step further and say our salvation is our epidural.

"will NOT escape": In the Greek text, before translation, Paul uses an emphatic double negative here, a construction he uses only four times in all his writings to stress his point.

Read 1 Thessalonians 5:4-5

"darkness"—believers no longer live in darkness, nor are they of the darkness.

Because we have the light of Christ and the knowledge of his return, we will not be surprised when it happens. The timing may not be known to us, but when those trumpets sound, we will know exactly what is happening.

Read 1 Thessalonians 5:6-7

"asleep"—nonbelievers are spiritually insensitive.

We as believers have a difficult time communicating with them because they are so one dimensional. They can't understand anything having to do with one's spirituality. This part of them is 'asleep'.

"be awake" or "be alert"—keep watch for Christ's return.

"sober" or "self-controlled"—in contrast with vs. 7 which describes someone with no self-control and the things they do in darkness.

Read 1 Thessalonians 5:8

"the day"—believers live in the light, using self-control to remain in the light of Christ.

"breastplate" and "helmet"—Paul often uses metaphors of armor for battle when talking about Christians. Here he is saying the 'equipment' we need for battling the darkness in the world is love, faith, and hope of salvation.

Read 1 Thessalonians 5:9

"appoint"—God's appointment versus man's choice is the point made here. God's wish is for all of mankind to receive salvation, but He gives us the ability to 'choose' to suffer wrath instead.

Read 1 Thessalonians 5:10

"awake or asleep"—alive or dead;

We know Paul is not using the same meaning here as in verse 6 where he uses awake and asleep to mean 'awakened to spiritual things' or 'spiritually insensitive' because those who are spiritually insensitive will not "live together with Him."

"with Him"—to be Christ's is to have entered a relationship that nothing can destroy.

Read 1 Thessalonians 5:11

"build each other up"—strengthen each other by supporting each other in the faith and love of Christ. Paul knows the Thessalonians are already doing this.

Read 1 Thessalonians 5:12

"those who work hard among you"—possibly means the church leaders.

Read 1 Thessalonians 5:13

"because of their work"—not just because they are your teachers, but respect them and appreciate them because they work hard for the Lord.

Read 1 Thessalonians 5:14

"those who are idle"—as we learned in the last chapter, some of the Thessalonians were so sure Christ was returning soon they gave up their jobs in order to prepare for it, depending on the other Christians to support them. But Paul says they should continue to work to support themselves. He also may be speaking of those who do nothing to help within the church, but rather sit back and allow others to do the work while they "warm the pews" and await the Lord's return.

"disruptive"—often those who sit idly by and allow others to do the work are also those who complain the most. They think they know how things should be done, but are not willing to it and grumble about the performance of others.

"the timid, the weak"—these are to be helped, not rejected, by those who are stronger. I believe he's speaking, not only of those who are physically weak, but also of those who are timid and weak in their faith.

Read 1 Thessalonians 5:15

"pays back"—retaliation is NEVER a Christian option. Christians are called to forgive.

Read 1 Thessalonians 5:16-17

People are naturally happy on some occasions, but a Christian's joy does not depend on circumstances. It comes from what Christ has done for us and is constant (or should be), as should our prayer be continuous.

Read 1 Thessalonians 5:18

No matter what the circumstances, no matter how bad things seem, Christians are to be thankful at all times because of what God has done for us in sending His Son and giving us hope.

Read 1 Thessalonians 5:19

"Spirit" or "Spirit's fire"—There is a warmth, a glow, about the Spirit's presence that makes this language appropriate. The kind of conduct that might 'put out the Spirit's fire' are things such as immorality and laziness. These are the two things Paul stresses most in his letters. There are other things, but these are the ones he addressed that applied most to the Thessalonians.

Read 1 Thessalonians 5:20

As Paul continues, we see he could be warning against a mechanical attitude towards worship which would discourage the expression of the gifts of the Spirit in the local assembly and would serve to smother the Spirit's fire.

Read 1 Thessalonians 5:21-22

Just because someone approves of the scriptures and claims to speak in the name of the Lord doesn't mean they should be accepted without question. Paul does not say what kind of test to apply, but in the very least, their teachings should agree with Paul's teachings.

Read 1 Thessalonians 5:23

This is typical of Paul's prayers. He often refers to God as a God of peace, or a similar phrase at the end of his prayers.
"your whole spirit, soul and body"—Paul is emphasizing the entire person.

We should try to keep our bodies, spirits and souls prepared for Christ's eventual return.

…Side Note: When studying this lesson, I was attempting to discern the difference in "spirit" and "soul." A feeling came over me—when I thought the word "soul", I felt a warmth or strength (difficult to describe) throughout my entire body, from head to toe. When I thought the word "spirit", the warmth or light (a feeling of joy—also difficult to describe) was only felt in my center, in my chest cavity (not only my heart, but my entire chest.) The difference between soul and spirit is much more than "a feeling". This was simply my experience when I was considering these differences. But now that I've mentioned it, I will briefly explain the difference.

The soul is earthly, or finite, and the spirit is heavenly, or eternal. The word "soul" means "life," or "living being." God breathed life into man and beast. When the soul leaves the body, we die. We *are* souls, living beings. We *have* eternal spirits. The spirit survives death. Our spirit is what gives us the ability to connect with God, who is Himself Spirit.

Read John 4:24

Read Hebrews 4:12

Here the scripture also relates them to "thoughts" vs. "intents of the heart." Have you noticed that sometimes your mind is telling you one thing, but your heart leads you in another direction? The same can be true of the soul and spirit.

Read 2 Corinthians 5:17

Knowledge of God is received and interpreted by the spirit. When we receive salvation, it is our spirit that is born again, reborn from above. Yet, we spend our lifetime perpetually cleansing our souls as we learn and grow and change our earthly habits. We will always be imperfect sinful beings, but we are cleansed by the shed blood of Christ and we have hope through God's infinite forgiveness through His grace. We "die daily" and are "reborn daily" in Christ.

Read 1 Corinthians 15:31

When I pray for guidance from the Holy Spirit, I don't hear voices or have any kind of visions. But once in a while something reveals itself in the strangest way.

Back to the letter to the Thessalonians…

Read 1 Thessalonians 5:24

Paul has confidence God can be relied upon to complete what He started. He WILL return as promised.

F.A.C.T.S.

Read 1 Thessalonians 5:25

We all need prayer constantly, not only when we are in trouble.

Read 1 Thessalonians 5:26

Paul is sending his love to all of them. Today we might say "Give everyone a hug for me." A kiss between same sexes was a normal greeting of that day—'holy kiss' meant kiss of love (more caring than your everyday greeting).

Read 1 Thessalonians 5:27

"I charge you"—this is very strong language. Paul is not simply requesting, but ORDERING they be sure all the members of the church hear this letter and know of his concern and advice for them.

This shows that Paul intended his letters to be used in the churches to help teach, just as we still use them today.

Read 1 Thessalonians 5:28

Paul always ends his letters with a blessing of grace for his readers.

2 Thessalonians – Chapter 1

The light tone Paul used in his first letter is gone in this one, which was written only a few weeks or months later. The Thessalonians had misunderstood portions of his first letter, so he is more stern and direct when writing this one. The good news Paul had received from Thessalonica was that the church members were continuing to grow in their faith. But the bad news was that false teachings about Christ's return were spreading, leading many of them to quit their jobs and wait idly for the end of the world.

Read 2 Thessalonians 1:1

This letter is written by Paul, on behalf of himself, Silas, and Timothy who were together in Corinth. It is written to the church in Thessalonica as a follow-up of his first letter.

Silas: In Greek, the name was Silvanus, a variant of Silas

Read 2 Thessalonians 1:2-4

Paul begins his letter with praise, showing he still has great love and respect for them.

The Greek word used here, which was translated as

"brothers and sisters" was *adelphoi* and refers here to believers, both men and women, as part of God's family. As Christians, we should always attempt to build up and encourage fellow believers.

Paul is aware of the difficulties they are enduring because of their faith and lets them know how proud he is of their perseverance. The key to surviving trials is perseverance and faith. When we are faced with crushing problems, we should have faith that God is using our trials for our good and for His glory.

Read 2 Thessalonians 1:5

Paul tries to give them encouragement. Although it may not be evident while they are being persecuted, God will reward them for their steadfastness and punish their persecutors.

Some people believe trials are a result of lack of faith or punishment for not living the way God wants us to. Paul is saying trials are a way of strengthening us and our perseverance is what will make us worthy of God's kingdom. Our problems can help us look upward rather than inward and provide us with opportunities to comfort others facing similar trials. How we react to our troubles can be an indicator of the strength of our faith, either helping or harming our testimony as Christians.

Knowing God is fair and just will give us patience in our suffering because we know He has not forgotten us. In His perfect timing, he will release us from our suffering. We need to trust in His timing.

Read 2 Thessalonians 1:6-10

The believer's victory will be when Christ returns. That is when we will see justice served.

"when the Lord Jesus is revealed from heaven in blazing fire with his powerful angels." What an image! In 1 Thessalonians, Paul mentions Christ's return, but here he gives a more powerful image of that event. The fire illustrates the Lord's wrath and vengeance toward the disobedient.

So many times we hear people ask the question, "Why do bad things happen to good people?" or "Why does God allow people to profit from their wrongdoing?" Paul's answer to that question would probably be, "It's only temporary." His conviction was that one day God would turn the tables on the unfairness of life. Our reward will be revealed in the future. We must remain steadfast in our faith for now.

The *"everlasting destruction"* Paul describes here is the place of eternal separation from God. Those separated from God in eternity no longer have any hope for salvation.

Read 2 Thessalonians 1:11-12

God's *"calling"* is for us to become like Christ. This is a lifelong and gradual process that will not be completed until we see Christ face to face. In order to be *"worthy"* of this calling, we need to strive to be as much like Christ as possible. That is our goal. We cannot achieve perfection in this world, but we need to be moving in that direction by allowing God to work in us.

An old proverb: "If you ask the wrong question, you will get the wrong answer."

When it comes to sin, we often ask the wrong question. When we ask the "is it wrong if..." questions, what we are really saying is "how much can I sin without it being labeled a sin by others?"

F.A.C.T.S.

Examples:

- A young couple wants to know how much sexual contact they can get away with before marriage and still not be sinning.

- A business man asks how many corners he can cut on his taxes and it not be considered cheating.

- A woman wants to know if it's okay to "share" some "facts" about someone so we can all pray for them.

- A man wants to know if it is a sin to utter a profanity when you bang your shin.

- A man wants to know if it is a sin if he was born with a bad temper and cannot control it.

- A teenager asks if her latest behavior is sin if "everyone is doing it" and other people don't think it's wrong.

In all of these instances, and others, there will be an ineffective or wrong answer because the wrong question is being asked.

Remember: If you have to wonder whether something is right or not, it's most likely wrong.

1 John 1:5 *This is the message we have heard from him and declare to you: God is light; in him there is no darkness at all.*

The things of God are "*light.*" They are not hidden in shadows or fog. What is right is plainly right, and the true seeker of righteousness will have no problem knowing what is right in God's eyes.

James 1:5 *If any of you lacks wisdom, you should ask God, who gives generously to all without finding fault, and it will be given to you.*

Psalm 18:28 *You, LORD, keep my lamp burning; my God turns my darkness into light.*

The Bible is abundantly clear on what is sin and what is not... lust, greed, gossip, selfishness, anger, pride, dishonesty, language, modesty, etc. The mature Christian quits playing the games of rationalization and calls sin for what it is. If something is NOT clearly and immediately righteous (according to God), then err on the side of holiness.

2 Thessalonians – Chapter 2

The word on the street was that Paul had said the last days had already arrived.

A few years ago thousands of people bought into one man's (Harold Camping) prediction that the "Rapture" was going to happen at a certain hour on a certain date (6pm on May 21, 2011). Many sold all they owned or gave it away to charity believing they would no longer need a home or their money.

This is exactly what was happening in Paul's day and was the reason for this letter. Church members were quitting work and sitting around watching the heaven's awaiting Christ's return because they either misunderstood what Paul had said or because there were false teachers spreading rumors using Paul's name.

NOTE: Matthew 24:36 says *"No one knows about that day or hour, not even the angels in heaven, nor the Son, but only the Father."*

Not even Jesus knows when He will return, only the Father knows.

Read 2 Thessalonians 2:1-4

Paul assures them the letter circulating with his name on it is a forgery. He also assures them the time has not yet come because before Jesus returns, there are several things which must occur including a rebellion and the revealing of the man of sin. Before Christ's return, there will be a great rebellion against God led by the antichrist, or man of sin.

Throughout history there have been evil individuals, but it is dangerous for us to try to label them as the antichrist in order to try to predict when Christ will return. Paul mentions the antichrist so we might be ready for anything that tests our faith. If we remain strong in our faith, we won't need to be fearful of what lies ahead because we know God is more powerful than this lawless man and has already defeated him. God has sealed the fate of all mankind and will be victorious in the end. It is our task to be prepared and spread the gospel so more people will be prepared.

Read 2 Thessalonians 2:5-7

The "secret" power of lawlessness is secret because no man can discover it. It can only be revealed by God. Scripture is not clear about who the restrainer is who holds back the lawless one, but only that he will not be restrained forever. However, we should not worry ourselves over the time when the restraint is lifted because God is far stronger than this man of sin and will save His people.

Although we have seen evil acts by many, we have never experienced the horror of complete lawlessness. This will happen when the "one who holds it back", possibly the Holy Spirit, is removed from the equation.

Paul is sometimes difficult to understand because he refers to things he may have verbally told them, which are not written down anywhere for us, leaving us somewhat in the dark.

Even Peter spoke of this in 2 Peter 3:15-16, one of the few instances where a New Testament writer mentions another New Testament writer.

He says, *"...and regard the patience of our Lord as salvation; just as also our beloved brother Paul, according to the wisdom given him, wrote to you, as also in all his letters, speaking in them of these things, <u>in which are some things hard to understand, which the untaught and unstable distort, as they do also the rest of the Scriptures, to their own destruction.</u>"*

Read 2 Thessalonians 2:8-12

The lawless one will use tricks and magic, false miracles, signs, and wonders to fool and deceive others to follow him. His powers will seem amazing, but his power comes from Satan. He will use his powers to destroy and lead people away from God. God's miracles always have a purpose of healing or helping and pointing us toward God. This is the litmus test we must remember when observing miraculous things.

Read 2 Thessalonians 2:13-14

Paul assures them they will know and share in the Lord's return.

"God chose you": Salvation begins and ends with God. We cannot do anything to purchase our salvation. It is a gift God has offered us, but we must accept His gift.

Read 2 Thessalonians 2:15

Paul asks them to stand firm in Christ's truth.

Read 2 Thessalonians 2:16-17

Paul tells them to receive encouragement and hope from God.

We shouldn't be afraid when we see the evil in this world increasing. God is still in control and guards us against Satan's attacks. We will have victory over evil by remaining faithful to God. We need to stand firm, keep working, and look forward to Christ's return. Being prepared for His return means spreading the gospel, reaching out to those in need, and building the Church. It is our responsibility to live for Him until the day of His return. If we are doing this, we will have no need to worry about the timing of that day because we will know and understand that God is still in control and will return when His time is right.

2 Thessalonians – Chapter 3

Paul begins chapter 3 by asking for prayer.

Read 2 Thessalonians 3:1-3

At that time Paul was in trouble in Corinth. His desire is for the Lord's message to be spread throughout the world. He asks them to pray for his safety from those who want to stop him from teaching the gospel. Then he asks them to pray for themselves, that the Lord will strengthen and protect them from evil.

If we arm ourselves with prayer daily, we can gain strength to win the struggle with the invisible powers waged against us during our daily routine.

In Acts 18:9-10, we learn Paul's prayer was answered.

"One night the Lord spoke to Paul in a vision: "Do not be afraid; keep on speaking, do not be silent. For I am with you, and no one is going to attack and harm you, because I have many people in this city."

Paul continues:

Read 2 Thessalonians 3:4-5

Paul is always attempting to encourage his fellow believers to stand strong and continue to do what is right. For us to do so, we must recognize the fact that there is always a threat of spiritual attack, and we must take it seriously. Satan lies in wait to trip us whenever our guard is down. We must arm ourselves through prayer and through scripture and associate with those who believe as we do and live a spiritual life.

Read 2 Thessalonians 3:6-10

Paul has no patience for laziness. There were people who were taking advantage of the charitable disposition of the church by using the expectation of the immediate appearance of the Lord an excuse to abandon their jobs and claim their right to be supported by those within the church who had more money than they did.

Notice Paul said "unwilling to work" not "unable to work." He is speaking strictly about laziness here. Some countries actually live by this rule today: "If you don't work, you don't eat."

Read 2 Thessalonians 3:11

When people become idle with nothing to occupy their minds, they sometimes begin gossiping or sticking their noses into other people's business. That's what was happening within the church. Lack of activity leads to sin. These people were becoming a burden to the church and wasting time that could have been used for helping others.

There is nothing wrong with relaxation. There is a time for rest, and a time for work. That is what gives our lives balance. Too much of either one is destructive. Do all you can to provide for yourself and your dependents, then rest.

Read 2 Thessalonians 3:12-13

Paul reminds them to keep working hard until Jesus returns and use their time wisely.

Read 2 Thessalonians 3:14

Although Paul was an advocate for charity toward those who truly were in need and spent a great deal of time gathering offerings for the poor, he spared no words condemning the able-bodied who could work, but would not. Here he forbids the brethren to support such people and commands the church to withdraw fellowship from them.

There is nothing in the Scripture or in the teachings of Christ to encourage charity to able-bodied lazy men whose profession is begging.

Read 2 Thessalonians 3:15

Even when we feel it necessary to disassociate ourselves from someone because of their evil ways, we should still show them love. We can distance ourselves without being rude or ugly. Paul suggests they tell the person why they are withdrawing their fellowship in a loving way. Paul was not advising cruelty or coldness, but the kind of 'tough love' we would show a brother or sister. We can show compassion while speaking the truth in love. He was being somewhat crafty by advising them to stop supporting these people; hunger and loneliness can be very effective ways to force someone to become productive.

Read 2 Thessalonians 3:16-18

Paul ends his letter by reminding them how all his letters will be in his own hand so they may distinguish them from the fake letters that were circulating with his name on them.

If you find your nose in other people's business, you may be underemployed. Look for a task to do for Christ or for your family, and get to work. You'll be happier, and so will those around you. Your life will become more complete. God didn't put us here to waste our time or live a useless life. He had a purpose for you when he created you. Find your purpose.

ND# The Letter to the

GALATIANS

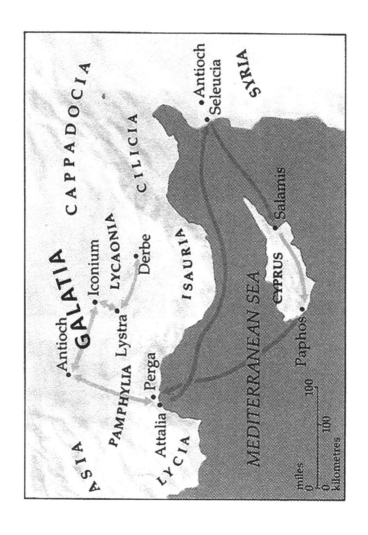

Written By
Paul Of Tarsus

In order to understand the book of Galatians, we must understand what Paul was facing.

The area on the map known in the 1st century as Galatia is today's country of Turkey. It helps to know where Paul's story takes place.

Paul went to Galatia during his 1st missionary journey from A.D. 46 thru 49 and established the church. He and Barnabas went from Antioch to Cypress (Barnabas's home), then to Asia Minor. Their work had been extremely successful because great multitudes of mostly gentiles had enthusiastically accepted Christ.

But soon after Paul left Galatia, these Judaizers came along insisting gentiles could not be saved unless they obeyed all the Jewish laws. They also said Paul did not have the authority from God, and he was not to be listened to. The Galatians heeded these teachings with the same enthusiasm with which they'd first received Paul's message. Because they believed what the Judaizers were teaching, there was an epidemic of circumcision among the gentile Christians.

There are 2 terms here we need to understand before we can grasp what Paul faced:

Judaizers [jew'de iz ers]: a sect of circumcised Jewish Christians who were not willing to accept the teaching of the Apostles and insisted gentiles could not be saved unless they obeyed all the Jewish laws: such as circumcision, eating special foods, and celebrating Jewish feast days. They made it their business to visit and unsettle Gentile churches, teaching that in order to become a Christian, Gentiles must first become a Jewish Proselyte [pros'e lait] and keep the Jewish law. They were determined to stamp Christ with the Jewish trademark.

Jewish Proselyte: If a male, not born a Jew, wished to become a Jewish Proselyte, he could do so by being circumcised and observing the ceremonial law of the Jews; in some respects, this is likened to a foreigner becoming a citizen of our country.

Being circumcised was an outward tradition of cutting away the flesh which represented the cutting away of sin in order to become a part of the kingdom of God.

At this time, Christianity was considered a Sect or Branch of Judaism.

Paul was born around 8 A.D., making him a few years younger than Jesus. This means he was in his mid-20's when he was converted on the road to Damascus. By the time he took his 1st missionary journey to establish the churches throughout Galatia, he was about 38-40 years old.

The purpose of this letter was to try to put an end to the confusion being caused by the false teachers. It is believed Paul actually wrote this letter about 50 or 51 A.D. from Antioch. This would be after his visit to Galatia during his 1st missionary journey, and after attending the Jerusalem Council of 49 A.D.

There is some debate by theologians as to when he wrote this book, some saying he wrote it before the Jerusalem Council, and others say after. The reason I believe he wrote it after the Jerusalem Council is because he mentions in the first chapter that he spent 3 years after his conversion preaching before visiting Jerusalem the first time. Then in chapter 2 he says he revisited Jerusalem 14 years later, which would have placed him there during the Jerusalem Council. Since he mentions these visits in his letter, it makes sense to me that he wrote it after the council meeting. According to chapters 15 & 16 of Acts, after this meeting, the Jerusalem Council gave Paul a letter to take back to the churches. Paul revisited Galatia immediately before setting out on his second missionary journey (probably to deliver that letter), and then again before his third.

Sometime before his 2nd journey, he wrote 1 & 2 Thessalonians and this letter to the Galatians.

As we study this letter, we will notice 4 special features:
- It's a strong letter: Paul does not compromise. He writes in very strong language and supports his main theme with many different arguments.
- It's a loving letter: Paul shows all the concern and care of a great pastor.
- It's brief: It has been called a 'rough draft' for the book of Romans, which was written later in greater detail and developed more fully.
- It's memorable: It contains many phrases that stick in your mind.

Paul begins by re-explaining the gospel he taught them and by claiming his authority from God. He reiterates we are saved only by believing in Jesus Christ, not by obeying the law.

He goes on to say Christians are to live by the law of love, not the law of Moses. He makes sure they know, although it had been a necessary part of Jewish national life, circumcision was not a part of the Gospel of Christ and had absolutely nothing whatsoever to do with Salvation.

Why did it matter so much? What would it hurt (other than the obvious pain) for them to simply accept they had to be circumcised and let it go at that? Why do you think Paul insisted on setting them straight on this point?

If Paul had not fought back and had allowed the Judaizers to continue to lead the gentile Christians astray, then everything he had taught would have completely lost its meaning.

The gospel Paul wanted them to understand was that man is justified by faith in Jesus Christ—nothing more and nothing less—and man is sanctified not by legalistic works, but by the grace and power of Christ and the Holy Spirit.

It was the rediscovery of this basic message of the book of Galatians that brought about the Reformation of the church. Galatians was relied upon very strongly by Martin Luther and therefore is often referred to as "Luther's book." One of the key verses Martin Luther liked to rely on was 2:16:

"Know that a man is not justified by observing the law, but by faith in Jesus Christ. So we, too, have put our faith in Christ Jesus that we may be justified by faith in Christ and not by observing the law, because by observing the law no one will be justified."

Galatians – Chapter 1

As mentioned earlier, Galatia was a region in Central Asia Minor which is now known as Turkey. It included cities such as Iconium, Lystra, Derbe, and Antioch. Paul is writing to all the churches in this area. These were churches he had preached in, or helped establish, during his first missionary journey. The entire journey and the visiting of these areas is described in detail in chapters 13 & 14 of Acts.

The Judaizers were saying Paul had no authority from God and was not to be listened to… This letter is partly in response to that.

First Paul begins his letter with a Greeting.

Read Galatians 1:1-5

Paul introduces himself as being sent by Jesus Christ and God the Father, not by men.

He is re-iterating that his authority *is* from God.

He stresses that God raised Jesus from the dead. This is important because the resurrection is the central affirmation of the Christian faith and because Paul had actually SEEN the risen Christ for himself and therefore was qualified to be an apostle, even though he wasn't one of the original twelve.

Paul's conversion on the road to Damascus, which is recorded in Acts chapter 9, was after Jesus had been crucified. Prior to that, he was a self-appointed tormentor and hired assassin whose main purpose was to hunt down and kill the followers of Jesus. This is probably the best example of how God can take the most despicable people and change their hearts and lives so He can use them to further His kingdom. So when we are asked to do something outside of our comfort zone, we might think we are not worthy and use this excuse to turn down the task.

We should never turn down an opportunity to serve. It may be God molding us and teaching us the way He wants us to live for Him.

Paul is not alone when he writes this letter. He writes, *"and all the brothers with me."*

He has others with him who agree with what he is writing.

He then identifies the people to whom he is writing: the people within the churches of Galatia. He greets them by wishing them grace and peace from God and the Lord Jesus Christ.

Remember, the entire gospel he has been preaching is all about God's grace and the peace Christ gives us.

He glorifies Christ here and once again uses this opportunity to emphasize what Christ did for us: gave himself for our sins so we may be rescued from the evil in this world; and this was all a part of God's plan and done according to His will.

Now Paul moves on to express the Purpose for this letter.

Read Galatians 1:6-10

Paul is surprised that these fellow Christians could be so fickle, turning so quickly from what he has taught them about Christ to the new teachings of the false teachers. He can't believe they would be so quick to desert God, who sent Christ so we could be saved through grace rather than by works and deeds, as these Judaizers were teaching.

He tells them that these false teachings are not any kind of gospel. Gospel means 'good news' and the things these Jews were teaching were basically the same 'old news' that had been taught for centuries. He tells them these false teachers are trying to confuse them and are distorting and misrepresenting the gospel of Christ. He is saying here that anyone, including himself or even an angel from heaven, who preaches anything other than the true gospel of Christ, should be eternally condemned—not just reprimanded—but thrown into the fires of hell for eternity.

When letters were written back then, they didn't have **BOLD** print or *italics* to stress their point. So if something was important, they would simply repeat it. The more times it was repeated, the more importance it held. So you notice here, Paul repeats himself by saying "And I say again, if anyone preaches a gospel other than what I taught you, let him be eternally condemned!"

So here we see we need to be extremely careful of what we teach to others about the gospel. If we get it wrong and go around telling people something that is not Biblical, we are guilty of the same thing these Judaizers were doing.

James 3:1 tells us teachers will be judged more harshly. This is what Paul is saying here.

He says, "take a good look at me. Does it look like I'm trying to please men? If I were trying to please men, I would be preaching what they want to hear. I wouldn't be traveling around trying to convince people about Christ and being chased out of cities and taking the risk of being imprisoned or beaten so I can be a servant of Christ." But he says he is a servant of Christ, again re-iterating his authority from God.

Paul gives his testimony concerning how he received the gospel message.

Read Galatians 1:11-17

Paul says that he, nor any other man, made up the gospel he preaches.

The gospel message was simple: "Salvation is for all and is received by faith in Christ."

He says no one taught him these things. He received his knowledge from revelations from Jesus Christ himself.

Here he confesses to, and reminds them, of his past, how he persecuted Christians and tried with wholehearted zeal to destroy the church of God. He says he was very knowledgeable about Judaism, more so than anyone else at his age at the time and believed completely in traditions of the Jews. When Paul was only 12 or 13 years old, he was schooled in Jewish law by one of the most knowledgeable Rabbis of that time.

Paul says God had chosen him before birth to be His servant. He had 'set him apart', not because Paul had done anything special, but strictly because of God's grace. God had, in His own time, revealed His Son to Paul so he could teach about Jesus to the Gentiles (the Greek word used here translates literally to "nations" or "people" who were designated foreigners.

In this case, they would have meant pagans or non-Jews).

And Paul said he didn't go to any man to see what he should do. He only listened to God and received his message from God.

The Judaizers were saying Paul was not an original apostle, but received his teachings from the twelve apostles and was merely repeating what he had heard them say. Paul says he didn't even go to Jerusalem and talk to the apostles of Christ to get their opinion. They were apostles before he was, but he didn't need their blessing, he already had God's blessing and God's grace.

How can we prepare ourselves for the times in our future when we will hear a distorted message about Christ?

- Through Bible study we can know when it is a distorted message.
- Through prayer, the Holy Spirit will help guide us to know the truth.
- Cling to the Word of God, rather than things we may have heard or been taught in the past, even if it was taught by people we thought to be Christians.

When we hear someone teaching untruths, should we argue with the messenger or condemn him in front of others?
- No, we should take him aside, show him from the Bible where he is wrong, try to persuade him into the truth so he can go back and correct his wrong teaching.
- If this does not work, then we should separate ourselves from him and his teachings.

Ponder on this: When Paul says God had chosen him from birth (while in his mother's womb) to be His servant. God had 'set him apart', what do you think this meant? Is Paul talking about predestination of certain individuals, or are we all chosen from birth and simply need to heed the call? To help understand Paul's intent, Read 1 Corinthians 12:4-11, Romans 8:28-30, and Ephesians 1:3-14. Pray for the Holy Spirit to guide you and help you understand. Try not to rely on what others have told you. Read and study for yourself so you'll know when you're hearing something untrue.

Read Titus 2:11

It would be difficult to interpret that verse any other way, no matter what is written before or after it. Now what do you believe Paul meant? Was he talking about 'predestination of certain individuals' or are we all chosen from birth and simply need to heed the call?

On the surface, sometimes it seems the Bible is contradicting itself. But God does not change. God is steadfast & unwavering. He does not and will not contradict Himself. So if it appears the scripture is inconsistent or conflicting, then we know we must be misinterpreting it.

That's when we need to dig deeper and possibly even go back to the original Hebrew or Greek to see what was intended.

Obviously, God has a plan and has chosen certain people to carry out that plan, such as Abraham, Moses, Ruth, David, and of course, Mary, among many others throughout history. I believe Paul felt God had chosen him in this same way. However, Paul still had 'free will' the same as we all do. He could have chosen to ignore God and continue his path of persecuting Christians.

God may not choose us for an earth-shattering part of His plan in the same way He did in the scriptures, but we don't have any way of knowing what His plan is for us unless we listen to the Holy Spirit and follow our calling.

God knew us all, even before we were born. It is up to each of us, using the free will He gave us, to decide if we will live God's will for us, or follow our own will. His wish is for all to be saved through His Son, Jesus Christ. That is why He sent Him. God did not make us robots to do His bidding; but gave us 'free will' to decide for ourselves which path to follow.

Paul's message was for all of us. His purpose was to make sure everyone heard the Gospel and had the opportunity to answer God's call to salvation.

Read Galatians 1:18-24

After being in Arabia and then going to Damascus, Paul spent three years preaching the gospel before he decided to go get acquainted with Peter (A.K.A. Cephas).

He stayed with him for 15 days, probably rejoicing in their shared love of Jesus.

He's letting these people know he received the gospel from Christ and had taught it in Damascus for three years ***before*** he ever met any of the apostles. So he couldn't have received his knowledge of Christ from them.

NOTE: His time in Arabia is not talked about in Acts, but it is believed Paul had been so stunned by his visit from Jesus and the new knowledge he had been given, he needed a time of solitude to absorb it all.

It was in Arabia that many of his revelations came. God was preparing him for his calling. He lets the people of Galatia know this time in Arabia was not some kind of summit meeting or conspiracy to come up with a story, he never even saw any of the other apostles. But he did see James (Jesus's brother, not the apostle James.) At this time, James was the leader of the elders in the Jerusalem church.

Paul assures them, in the name of God, he is being completely truthful.

When he left Peter, he went to Syria and Cilicia (in Tarsus, Paul's home). He didn't go to these places to see anyone. He went there to preach. He says no one in Syria or Cilicia knew him. He was a total stranger to the Christian Jews there. This was his home, but he'd been gone for a very long time. And when he'd lived there before, he didn't associate with Christians.

Even though he was a stranger to them, these people had heard of Saul, the man who had persecuted Jews who had become Christians, and they had heard of his conversion and how he was now preaching Christ's gospel. So they welcomed him and praised God for him.

I imagine those years between his conversion and when he went to see Peter, he had felt pretty alone in trying to preach the message that Christ had given him to teach. So imagine how good this made him feel, to be finally accepted in his home town among a group of people who already knew Christ.

We can get a small sampling of this joy when we find a church that welcomes us and has the same faith we do. Anyone who says they don't need church is going it alone much in the same way Paul did for those three years. It can be done, but it's so much easier and more joyful when you can share your faith with others of the same faith.

F.A.C.T.S.

Galatians – Chapter 2

In chapter 1, Paul told about visiting Peter in Jerusalem and meeting James. He explained he had already been preaching the gospel several years before meeting these men. Therefore, he could not have received the gospel from them as the false teachers had claimed.

Read Galatians 2:1-7

Here, Paul continues to explain that it was 14 years later before he returned to Jerusalem, and Barnabas and Titus had gone with him.
- Barnabas's given name was Joseph, and he was a Levite from the island of Cyprus. He had been Paul's companion on the first missionary journey.
- Titus was a Gentile and a Christian who served as Paul's delegate to Corinth and was later left in Crete to oversee the church there. Paul had a specific reason for taking Titus with him on this trip; he wanted to see how the leaders of the church accepted Titus since he was a Gentile who had not been circumcised.

Paul went to the leaders of the church (probably James, Peter, and John) to explain to them what he had been preaching and to confer with them. He was beginning to feel as if all he had taught had been in vain because the churches were already beginning to listen to the false teachers. He was looking for moral support and advice from fellow Christians.

Even the leaders of the church in Jerusalem must have agreed with him concerning the old law not needing to be followed anymore because Titus, who was a Greek, had been accepted as a Christian without circumcision.

The Judaizers had entered into the church and tried to convince everyone that in order to be saved, you had to first be a Jew. If you were a Gentile, then you had to be circumcised to convert. So Paul is saying by doing this, these Judaizers were taking away the freedom God was trying to give us from the slavery of the old law. Jesus Christ freed us from those laws when he died on the cross. We need only to believe and accept the grace of God for salvation, not live by a lot of superseded laws.

Paul says none of them believed what the Judaizers were teaching and all the leaders were in agreement. They didn't even hesitate for one minute to throw out these ideas because they knew it wasn't what Jesus had intended.

As for these leaders of the church with whom he had conferred, (Peter, James, and John), it didn't matter that they had been important people within the church, they had not added anything to the gospel he had already been teaching. They believed the same as he did.

In the Greek, the word used here for Gentiles meant "the uncircumcised," and the word used here for Jews meant "the circumcised."

In fact, they had agreed with all of what he had taught. They understood it was his job to preach to the Gentiles just as it was Peter's job to teach the gospel to the Jews. This is not to say Paul didn't preach to Jews at all. In fact, he usually went to the synagogue first whenever he arrived in a city. But he did consider himself to be foremost an apostle to the Gentiles.

F.A.C.T.S.

Read Galatians 2:8-10

This job had been given them by God, and God was leading them both in their ministries—Paul's to the Gentiles, and Peter's to the Jews.

Peter's Greek name was Cephas, which meant "stone or rock" in Aramaic. So the original Greek manuscript of this letter had Peter's name as Cephas. It was translated as "Peter" because the Greek Petros and the Latin Petrus means "rock."

Pillars was a common metaphor used during that time for those who represent and strongly support an institution. These 'pillars' of the church had recognized Paul and Barnabas as fellow Christians. The 'right hand of fellowship' was a common practice during that time among both Hebrews and Greeks indicating a pledge of friendship. We still use this ritual today in a handshake.

The leaders had agreed they should continue their work teaching the Gentiles, but asked they also remember and help the Jews who were poor. This was a strong commitment within the church and was believed to be among the most important work of the church—to take care of the poor and downtrodden. But Paul says he was planning to do that anyway.

Read Galatians 2:11-14

Antioch was the leading city in Syria and the third leading city of the Roman empire. Paul had left from this city for each of his missionary journeys, so it was home base for him.

Peter had come to Antioch when he heard about the Judaizers and had tried to make peace by urging the Gentiles to "simply go along with the circumcision so everyone would be happy." He hadn't intended to go against the gospel. He had only wanted to appease the Judaizers. But in doing this, Paul felt he was compromising the gospel message and he told him so to his face.

Paul points out that Peter used to fellowship with the Gentiles until James sent some of the Jews from Jerusalem. Upon their arrival, suddenly Peter separated himself from the Gentiles and began hanging out with the Judaizers so these important people from the leading church in Jerusalem would see he was a good Jew. He knew the Judaizers were wrong in their teachings, but he was afraid to go up against them.

There are preachers doing this today. They don't always agree with the church associations, but must abide by what they say. Or they are afraid to preach certain sermons from the pulpit for fear of upsetting some church members. For centuries, governments have dictated to church leaders what they may preach and what they cannot. This is happening on a small scale in the United States, so we must be on our guard that it doesn't escalate into a larger problem.

Paul says Peter was being a hypocrite by going along with these Judaizers because he knew better and was teaching something he didn't even believe in. And not only that, but the Christian Jews were listening to him and joining him in the hypocrisy. And now Barnabas was listening to the lies too. Peter was an important leader in the church of Jerusalem, so why shouldn't they believe what he was teaching?! We want to believe we can trust in the teachings of the church leaders, but we should be careful to study the Word ourselves so we can know if they are teaching something incorrectly.

Paul, in front of all the others within the church, tries to reason with Peter and let him know what he is doing is wrong. He says "Hey, YOU'RE a Jew, but YOU don't live by the old laws. So why do you make the Gentiles live by the Jewish laws?"

When we disagree with someone in the church, do we go to that person? More often than not, it happens this way: This person gets mad at that person (it can be either a church leader or a fellow member). The person who gets mad picks up the phone and begins calling their friends. The person they are mad at is filleted and fried over and over again.

That is NOT the way a faithful follower of Jesus will treat anyone. The Apostle Paul got very upset with a Christian brother. He was upset because Peter had not acted as he should. Paul, however, did not run around telling this one and that one about it. What he wanted to say ABOUT Peter he said TO Peter.

I suggest the next time we get upset with or want to criticize someone, we need to ask ourselves a couple of questions.

- "Am I so sure what I am upset or critical of is valid enough to say to the person's face without fear of being proven wrong?"
- "If it is valid, then shouldn't I be talking to the person face to face instead of talking about the person behind their back?"

Read Galatians 2:15-19

Paul does not condemn the law of the Jews. In Romans 7:12, Paul says "So then, the law is holy, and the commandment is holy, righteous and good." He believes these laws were given to them by God and therefore it is holy, righteous, and good, but he is arguing against the illegitimate use of the Old Testament laws, which made the observance of those laws the grounds of acceptance with God. The law doesn't make men right with God. Only through faith are we justified, which is the essence of the gospel message.

In Romans 3:20 & 3:28, Paul says *"Therefore no one will be declared righteous in his sight by observing the law; rather, through the law we become conscious of sin."* and *"For we maintain that a man is justified by faith apart from observing the law."*

While we are seeking justification, we obviously will discover how sinful we really are; does this mean that Christ validates sin? Of course not.

Paul is saying if he accepts the law has to be obeyed in order to be saved, then he will be convicted by the old law because he has not obeyed it. It is humanly impossible for us to obey all of the laws all of the time.

There are 613 Mitzvot (Commandments), which cover almost every aspect of life. Laws about:
- using the name of God (which they will not even spell out; they write it as G-d.),
- honoring and handling of the Torah,
- symbols required for them to either wear or display,
- how to pray,
- keeping the brotherhood and loving others,
- laws about helping the poor and needy,
- laws regarding treatment and association with gentiles,
- laws regarding marriage, divorce, and family,
- even laws on sexual relations!

Their laws also included:
- how to measure time and how to observe their feast days and other holy days and times of the year.
- There were a list of dietary laws,
- business practice rules,
- how to treat employees, servants, and slaves,
- laws about vows, oaths, and swearing.

All of these listed are only 14 of the 34 sections of laws covering everything from prophecy and offerings and taxes to breeding of animals and sowing seed to how to treat enemies in times of peace and times of war.

Paul says he gave up concentrating on keeping laws so he could focus more on living for God. If we are spending every minute of our life worrying about keeping laws, we cannot focus on living our lives for God's service. Therefore, we become "slaves of the law."

Read Galatians 2:20-21

This is a another key verse! By accepting Christ through faith, he has given up living his life for himself and turned his life over to Christ, to do His will and be His servant. He does this because Christ loved him enough to die on the cross for him.

If we ignore the gospel message which says we are saved by faith and believe we are saved by obedience to the law, then Christ died for nothing! Paul is saying if we are saved by the law, and not by grace, then this makes a complete mockery of the cross.

Obviously, circumcision is not a hotly debated subject today, but how is Paul's message still relevant? Many people still believe man's ability to get into heaven depends on how many rules he keeps and how respectable he is. Paul shows us what counts is FAITH, not works.

So if works isn't important in getting into heaven, why can't we just live the way we want? The freedom a Christian obtains through acceptance of Christ is not the freedom to live as we please. It only frees us from obeying laws that have nothing to do with salvation, such as circumcision or not eating pork, and the 611 other Old Testament laws. When we become Christians, we will not be motivated by our own selfishness, but by our desire to express the joy and comfort we receive from the Holy Spirit in our character, behavior, and relationships.

Read Romans 6:14

Christ is the end of the Law and believers are not under the Mosaic Law. New Testament believers are not under Law but under grace.

Read Romans 8:2-4

Since the Lord Jesus Christ fulfills the Law by His person and work, believers are under a new law; the obligation to walk by the Spirit through faith.

Galatians – Chapter 3

This chapter is among my favorites in the Bible. It explains the promise from God, which allows us to become His children.

My granddaughter used to pretend she was a princess. I explained to her that Jesus is the King of Kings, and we are God's children, therefore she IS a princess. We who have accepted His gift of salvation are all princes and princesses, heirs of the Kingdom.

In this letter, Paul is astounded that the people in Galatia were turning away from his teachings so quickly simply because some Judaizers had come into the churches and were teaching that in order to be saved, you had to be Jewish or converted to a Jew.

This completely invalidated everything Paul had taught them.

Read Galatians 3:1-5

Paul is upset with those who are listening to the Judaizers. He asks 'how can you be such fools as to believe what they are teaching? Jesus was crucified! You know this!'

Paul asks, "How did you receive the Holy Spirit anyway? By observing the old laws? No, by believing what I taught you; you heard the good news and you believed it." Again he asks them how they can be so foolish. They've experienced the Holy Spirit, so what is it they think they can accomplish by turning back to the old ways?

Trying to achieve righteousness by works, including circumcision, was part of life in the flesh. After receiving the Holy Spirit, we no longer should be living life in the flesh, but in the Spirit.

Paul asks, "Why have you suffered the ridicule if it meant nothing?" Again he asks how they received the Holy Spirit in the first place—was it by obeying the law of Moses or through belief in Jesus Christ?

Paul mentions the Holy Spirit 16 times in this letter to the Galatians.

Read Galatians 3:6-9

Paul is referring to Scripture from Genesis 15:6: "Abram believed the LORD, and he credited it to him as righteousness." He says to remember Abraham and how he believed God, and God rewarded him with righteousness.

Abraham was the physical and spiritual father of the Jewish race. So how can these Gentiles be descendants of Abraham? If you believe, you become a child of Christ, and therefore become a descendant of Abraham.

Paul again refers to the Scriptures. Genesis 12:3 says, *"I will bless those who bless you, and whoever curses you I will curse; and all peoples on earth will be blessed through you."*

God told Abraham *"All nations will be blessed through you"*

He didn't say all Jews, or all of your kin, he said ALL NATIONS. So we know from this God had a plan, even then, for all to be able to receive salvation

.

Paul suggests these Scriptures revealed God would save non-Jewish people through their faith. All who have faith are blessed just as Abraham was blessed because of his faith. By believing, we are adopted into the family of Abraham, making us God's children through faith.

Read Galatians 3:10-14

Paul quotes scripture from Deuteronomy 27:26: *"Cursed is the man who does not uphold the words of this law by carrying them out." Then all the people shall say, "Amen!"*

If you rely on the law for your salvation, you cannot be saved. For the Scriptures say if you disobey even one of the laws, you are cursed.

Paul then refers to the Scripture found in Habakkuk 2:4: *"See, he is puffed up; his desires are not upright—but the righteous will live by his faith"*

So it's obvious no one could possibly be so perfect as to do everything the law requires. Habakkuk 2:4 says even when a person is puffed up (arrogant) or has sinful desires, thereby disobeying the law, he can still be righteous by living by his faithfulness.

God's blessing has never been earned, but has always been freely given. The law is not based on faith, far from it. The Scriptures say "*the man who does these things will live by them.*"

This is found in Leviticus 18:5: *"Keep my decrees and laws, for the man who obeys them will live by them. I am the LORD."*

Being very knowledgeable in the Scripture, Paul continues to quote more.

Deuteronomy 21:23: *"You must not leave his body on the tree overnight. Be sure to bury him that same day, because anyone who is hung on a tree is under God's curse. You must not desecrate the land the LORD your God is giving you as an inheritance."*

Christ released us from the curse of the law by becoming cursed for us, for the Scriptures say *"Cursed is everyone who is hung on a tree."* (The word translated as "tree" here originally meant stocks and poles on which bodies were impaled). Christ did this so the promise given to Abraham could come true, and all people (including Gentiles) could receive the promise of the Spirit through faith in Him.

Read Galatians 3:15-18

Here Paul tries to appeal to them by giving them an example with which they can identify. A 'human covenant' normally indicated a last will and testament.

In the Greek translation of the Old Testament, it had been used to indicate God's promise to His people. So this was an apt analogy and one they could understand.

Paul says no one can change or add to a last will and testament once it's been established, and the same is true with God's promise. Paul again refers to Genesis, when the Lord gave His promises to Abraham. The Scripture said the promises were spoken to Abraham and 'his seed', not plural, but one seed—one person—that one being Christ.

The law wasn't introduced until 430 years after God made this promise to Abraham and doesn't change the promise. God's 'will' could not be changed. The inheritance (being the blessing God gave to Abraham) was given by a promise, or covenant, from God and cannot be given or changed by the law.

Read Galatians 3:19-20

So if the law didn't change God's plan for salvation, then why was there a law given at all? It was given so men could understand right from wrong until the time when the seed, or special descendant of Abraham (which was

Christ) had come, fulfilling the promise.

The law was given through angels to a mediator (which was Moses).

The promise God had given to Abraham had stood at the center of God's relationship with his people (the Jewish people). After the exodus from Egypt, the law became an additional element in that relationship.

The law is what Jeremiah spoke of as the 'old covenant' and Christ was the 'new covenant'.

Paul says the law was given through angels.

There are several verses to back this up:

Deuteronomy 33:2 *He said: "The LORD came from Sinai and dawned over them from Seir; he shone forth from Mount Paran. He came with myriads of holy ones from the south, from his mountain slopes.*

Acts 7:38,53 *He was in the assembly in the desert, with the angel who spoke to him on Mount Sinai, and with our fathers; and he received living words to pass on to us…53you who have received the law that was put into effect through angels but have not obeyed it."*

Hebrews 2:2-3 *For if the message spoken by angels was binding, and every violation and disobedience received its just punishment, 3how shall we escape if we ignore such a great salvation? This salvation, which was first announced by the Lord, was confirmed to us by those who heard him.*

Moses was a mediator and was given the law in a formal arrangement of mutual commitments between God and Israel.

But the promise given to Abraham was given directly from God and involved no commitment from Abraham, only from God. No mediator was involved. Whenever there is only one side committing to something, with nothing in return by the other party, there is no need for a mediator.

So the law was purchased by commitment from the Israelites. The promise to Abraham was a 'gift' from God.

Read Galatians 3:21-24

So is the law a bad thing, going against God's will? No. The reason for the law is this: although it cannot save, it serves to reveal sin, which alienates God from man, and shows the need for the salvation the promise offers.

Before Christ (wherein lies our faith), we were prisoners of the law (or of sin), for the law revealed to us what sin was. And since no one could live without disobeying some of the laws, it exposed sin, yet gave us no way to be forgiven for that sin, making us prisoners. The law was "put in charge" to lead us to Christ—to understand this fully, we have to understand what this terminology meant in those days.

The Greek word used here was 'paidagogos' (ped i gog us) which was an attendant who accompanied a young boy to be sure he arrived at his intended destination safely, using discipline whenever necessary (a sort of guardian or baby-sitter). The (ped i gog us) paidagogos usually accompanied his charge to, and from, his teachers.

In this analogy, the teacher was Christ and the law was the guardian. Once the law (or guardian) had done its job and led us to Christ (our teacher), then it was possible for us to be justified by faith.

Read Galatians 3:25-29

Now that the law (or guardian) has safely delivered us to Christ (the teacher), the guardian is no longer needed. By faith we are adopted into God's family and therefore justified to be an heir with all the rights and privileges of a family member.

Unity in Christ transcends all distinctions such as ethnicity, sex, or social standing. We are all united in Christ, to be heirs of the promise. As such, we are all called to the great commission to spread the gospel and teach others about Christ. God didn't call only men, or only Caucasians, or just those of a certain social class to His service. All Christians are to serve Him.

Since Christ was of Abraham's lineage, and we are adopted as His children, then all Christians are Abraham's true, spiritual descendants, fulfilling the promise God made to Abraham. Because of this promise, we receive all of God's blessings.

Galatians – Chapter 4

Paul is continuing his thought from the previous chapter… all Christians are sons of God.

How are we God's children? Christ was Abraham's direct descendent. Through our faith in Jesus Christ we are adopted into the family and become heirs of the promise God made to Abraham.

Read Galatians 4:1-7

If a child (meaning a minor) inherits an entire estate, he still has nothing of his own, just as if he were a slave. A child is still under the control of his guardians and trustees until he becomes the age when he can actually inherit, the age set by what his father indicated in his will.

In the same way, before Christ, Christians were subject to the principles of the world.

The word 'principles' here refers to the fundamental forms of religion, both those of the Jews under the law and those of the Gentiles old religious beliefs. When he calls them 'principles of the world', he means these ideas of religion are of man and not of God.

But when the time had fully come… meaning the time set by God for his children to become adult heirs …he sent His Son, born of a woman... making Him human ...born under law... born at a time when Moses' law ruled the land, so He was also subject to the law the same as all other Jews at that time. Then he could redeem those that were still living under the law, so we could receive our full inheritance.

Once Jesus had completed His task to redeem God's children, He didn't leave us on our own. God knew we needed a way to communicate with Him and to know Him as our Heavenly Father. So He gave us the gift of the Holy Spirit to be our conduit (direct connection) with Him. This Spirit knows our Heavenly Father personally and therefore can help us know Him as our Father.

The term 'Abba' was used here, which indicates an extremely close relationship to God. As adopted children of God, we are heirs of the promise.

Read Galatians 4:8-16

Here we can feel Paul's frustration. He reiterates before they knew God, they were slaves to other humans and their rules. But now they know the one true God, and they realize the idols they'd worshipped before were not gods at all. They know God—or more importantly, are known by God—so how could they think of turning back to the old laws, which had made them so miserable? Paul asks them if they want to go back to living like that? He asks, "how could you go back to believing in those rituals and in the law, in good works, or in the cold, dead customs?" Why would you relapse into a second childhood when you should be enjoying the freedom of full-grown heirs?

He says they are observing special days (i.e. the Sabbath & Day of Atonement) and months and seasons (i.e. New Moons, Passover, & Firstfruits) and years (i.e. the Sabbath year) as required by the old law. The Pharisees diligently observed all these in order to gain merit before God—to make themselves worthy. Of course, Paul taught them these things had never been, nor could ever be, in themselves a means of salvation. He is frustrated and worries all his efforts to teach them the truth of Christ was completed wasted on them.

Is Paul saying it is wrong to observe holidays?

Read Romans 14:1-6

It isn't the observance of holidays that is the sin, but the REASON we celebrate. If we are doing it to gain favor with God so He will allow us into heaven, it is in vain. But He doesn't care if we enjoy ourselves. And we should not judge others for their customs. There is certainly nothing wrong with having family gatherings or fellowship with others to celebrate an occasion, as long as we understand we are not doing it to obey some Law.

Paul pleads with them. He says he was once just like them (believing in the old laws), and now he wants them to become like him (a child of Christ). He also lets them know he holds no ill-will toward them.

Here we see a little insight of what it was like when Paul had first gone to Galatia and preached to these people during his first missionary journey. He says an illness had caused him to go there to begin with, and then he preached the Gospel to them—probably speaking of his blindness after seeing Christ on the road to Damascus. But although this illness caused them discomfort and extra work, they had welcomed him and hadn't turned him away or looked down on him. Instead they welcomed him as if he were Jesus Christ Himself, or an angel from God.

So what happened to all that joy? When he had been with them, they had been so caring and loving that they would have torn out their own eyes and given them to him. So now, he asks, have they turned away from him because he spoke the truth to them?

Sometimes when we tell the truth, we risk the result of losing friendships. This is especially true when we stick to our convictions in the Lord rather than go along with the crowd.

Read Galatians 4:17-20

Because of the passion the Judaizers had for the message they were teaching, they were able to convince them of their false teachings. Paul explains it's okay to be so zealous, as long as you are zealous about the truth and about things with a good purpose. He also adds they should always be enthusiastic about the truths he taught them, even after he was gone.

Paul calls them 'his dear children' showing his deep affection for them. He also may be calling them children because they've slipped back into being children of the old law rather than adults in the Spirit. He is so pained by their turning away from the Gospel he compares it to the pain of childbirth and says the pain won't go away until they have turned back to Christ.

He tells them if he could be with them, maybe he would be able to understand them better, but he cannot comprehend why they're acting the way they are.

Read Galatians 4:21-27

Why would anyone who understands what the law says want to go back to living under it? But since they do want to be under the law of Moses, he uses it to make a point.

Paul then goes back to the old scriptures to remind them of the history of Abraham. He had two sons, one by a slave, who was Hagar, and the other by a free woman, who was Sarah.

The son of the slave, Ishmael, was born the same as anyone else. But the son of the free woman, Isaac, was born because of the promise God had made to Abraham.

Remember, Sarah was well past child-bearing years, so her conceiving a child was a true miracle.

Paul says this may be taken figuratively, not because it was not historical, but because he was going to use these true events to illustrate a theological truth. He explains these women represent the two covenants between God and men.

The first, (Hagar) the slave, is from Mount Sinai (origin of the law of Moses), and the children she bears will be slaves (slaves of the law) and form the present city of Jerusalem (meaning the city that is still ruled by Judaism and still under the bondage of the laws issued at Mount Sinai).

In contrast, Sarah, is free and is the mother of all Christians—those free from the law.

Read Galatians 4:28-31

Here Paul recites the scripture found in Isaiah 54:1. This is a joyful song from Isaiah about the promise to exiled Jerusalem. Jerusalem represents the 'Believers'.

Although it appeared they could conceive no 'children' or new believers, the promise was made by God that they would. Through the gospel of Christ, 'Jerusalem's children' have become many. Isaac was Abraham's true son, but we are like him in that we are heirs of the promise.

Isaac's half-brother Ishmael, who was born in the ordinary way, persecuted Isaac, who was born by the power of the Spirit.

Read Genesis 21:9-10

Paul says it is the same today. Those who are born of the law, the unsaved, will persecute those of us born in the Spirit who are saved. Here Paul again recites the scripture, using Sarah's words from Genesis 21:10 as Scriptural basis for teaching the Galatians to remove the Judaizers from the church. Paul says the scripture is clear. None of the slave woman's children will EVER share in the inheritance.

The believer is not enslaved to the law, but is a child of promise and lives by faith.

Many believe there is no connection between the Old and New Testaments and that they speak of two Gods with two different kinds of demands on men. But Paul demonstrates to us how they are related and how they prove to us it was all a part of God's ultimate plan. This should make us realize God's greatness and foresight and make us trust him more with our tiny little lives.

Other than freeing us from the law, how does our birth in Christ give us freedom?

Not only does it free us from the laws of Moses, but through our faith God gives us strength to face things which otherwise may defeat us, giving us a peace we would otherwise not know, which in turn gives us joy.

We should exhibit our joy in Christ so others might see His light shining through us. There is nothing more attractive to others than a happy and joyful countenance.

Proverbs 15:13 *A happy heart makes the face cheerful, but heartache crushes the spirit.*

Galatians – Chapter 5

Read Galatians 5:1-6

Paul says Christ has made us free from the law. Don't turn and go back into the slavery of the law. The Greek word used here meant to be 'caught up or entangled in.'

Paul then goes back to the issue at hand, circumcision. He tells them if they allow themselves to be circumcised, then Christ's sacrifice was for nothing! He then gives them a warning: if you allow yourselves to be circumcised because you believe in the law, then you must follow the ENTIRE law. You can't pick and choose which parts of the law you will obey. You either obey all of it or none of it.

Paul isn't saying we shouldn't obey any of the laws. Obviously God gave the law for good reason. But we mustn't obey the laws with the idea we will be saved by doing so. If we try to earn salvation through the law, then we will be cut out of the inheritance and we will fall from grace. Gaining God's favor by observing the law and receiving it by grace are mutually exclusive (meaning they cannot occur at the same time.) If you toss a coin once, the result is either heads or tails, but not both. It is the same with believing either in receiving God's favor through the law or by grace. Believing both is impossible.

We who believe and follow Christ have the true hope of righteousness, when we will receive God's final verdict of 'not guilty', which is assured to the believer by faith. We will be made right with God through faith. When a person is in Christ Jesus, it doesn't matter if he is circumcised or not. The only important thing is faith—the kind of faith which works through love. Faith is not mere intellectual acceptance, but a living trust in God's grace which expresses itself in acts of love.

I once got a fortune cookie that had a great description of "faith." It said, "Faith is a bird that feels the light and sings while the dawn is still dark." When our lives are at their darkest point, our faith is being tested. This is when we must be strong enough to allow God to carry our burdens and lead us through the darkness while we continue singing His praises. We may not be able to see the light, or God's presence, but we should feel it, like the bird, by having the faith it is there none the less.

Circumcision was always symbolic in the Bible, even in the Old Testament.

Read Deuteronomy 30:6

Paul actually uses this metaphor in Romans 2:29. He writes, *"No, a person is a Jew who is one inwardly; and circumcision is circumcision of the heart, by the Spirit, not by the written code..."*

Read Galatians 5:7-10

Paul says they were going the right direction and obeying the truth. Who persuaded them to stop? Whoever it was, was NOT from God. Then he warns, "Be careful! Just a little bit of yeast makes the entire batch of dough rise." Whenever 'yeast' is used as a symbol in the Bible, it indicates evil or false teaching. Paul is saying something small can become a very big problem.

Paul tells them he knows somebody is upsetting them with new ideas and whoever it is will be punished. He also says he trusts them NOT to believe those ideas.

Read Galatians 5:11-18

He uses the term "Brothers and sisters" which is an endearment showing Paul still loves these people as family. He makes the point if he was preaching circumcision, as the Judaizers were claiming he was, then why was he still being persecuted?

Paul then speaks of the embarrassment to the Jews who crucified Christ—if what the Judaizers were teaching was true, the Jews had done nothing wrong and would have no reason to be embarrassed by the crucifying of Christ.

Paul becomes a bit sarcastic here by saying he wishes these people who are upsetting them with their ideas would also insist on castration, meaning to cut themselves off.

In this context, the Greek word for flesh (sarx) refers to the sinful state of human beings, often presented as a power in opposition to the Spirit. This word is also used in verses 16, 17, 19, and 24, then again in chapter 6:8.

Just because you are not under the law does not mean for you to use your freedom as an excuse to do all the things your physical body wants. Instead, you must serve each other in love.

Paul quotes scripture found in Leviticus 19:18. *"The entire law is made complete in this one command: Love others the same as you love yourself."*

Seeking to attain God's acceptance through the law breeds self-righteousness and a critical spirit. How often do we find these traits in people?—where they are critical of others who aren't dressed just right or aren't 'their' type of people.

Live by following the Spirit. The Greek word used here for 'live' means habitual conduct, ongoing and consistent. Living by the power and guidance of the Spirit is the key to conquering sinful desires. Then you won't do those selfish and evil things you are tempted to do by your human nature. Human nature wants things which are against the Spirit; the Spirit wants things which are against human nature. These are two opposing forces. Because of this, you can't do whatever you want. But if you allow the Spirit to lead you, then you will not be condemned by the law.

Read Galatians 5:19-26

Paul lists some of the wrong, or sinful, acts caused by our human nature. He groups some of these together because they relate to each other in some way.

- committing sexual sins and impurity
- worshiping false gods and practicing witchcraft
- hating, jealousy, making trouble, becoming too angry, being selfish, causing divisions, and envying others
- orgies, wild parties, getting drunk, and other such things.

Paul says people who do these things will NOT inherit God's kingdom.

Other lists of vices of the human nature are found in 1 Corinthians 6:9-10: *"Or do you not know that wrongdoers will not inherit the kingdom of God? Do not be deceived: Neither the sexually immoral nor idolaters nor adulterers nor men who have sex with men nor thieves nor the greedy nor drunkards nor slanderers nor swindlers will inherit the kingdom of God."*

Note: The words "men who have sex with men" translate two Greek words that refer to the passive and active participants in homosexual acts. This is not "politically correct" today, but God's laws do not change at the whim of mankind.

Notice when Paul talks about the sinful nature, he uses the plural, "acts" here. Acts of the sinful nature is plural, indicating a division of different things. These things cause confusion and division among people.

When Paul lists the things produced by the Spirit, he uses the singular "fruit." Fruit, being one singular thing, indicates unity, a close tie between the things listed—a sort of bond. The use of the word 'fruit' was not accidental. These virtues grow within us when we are fed by the Spirit just as fruit is produced on trees. The Spirit produces: Love, joy, peace, patience, kindness, goodness, faithfulness, gentleness, and self-control. There is no law against these things.

Those who belong to Christ have nailed their own human nature to crosses, along with its feelings and selfish desires. Since we get life from the Spirit, we should follow the Spirit. The Greek word used here literally meant to 'walk in line with'. We must not be conceited or make trouble for each other. Neither should we be jealous of one another.

Other lists of virtues of the Spirit filled are found in Ephesians 4:2, Ephesians 5:9, and Colossians 3:12-15.

- Ephesians 4:2: "Be completely humble and gentle; be patient, bearing with one another in love."

- Ephesians 5:9: "…for the fruit of the light consists in all goodness, righteousness and truth…"

- Colossians 3:12-15: *"Therefore, as God's chosen people, holy and dearly loved, clothe yourselves with compassion, kindness, humility, gentleness and patience. Bear with each other and forgive one another if any of you has a grievance against someone. Forgive as the Lord forgave you. And over all these virtues put on love, which binds them all together in perfect unity. Let the peace of Christ rule in your hearts, since as members of one body you were called to peace. And be thankful."*

We need to concentrate in communicating and connecting more closely with the Holy Spirit so we can produce more virtuous fruit in our lives and character.

Galatians – Chapter 6

Paul continues his letter.

Read Galatians 6:1-3

Again Paul lets the Galatians know he still considers them 'Brethren' and is showing his love towards them by addressing them in this way. He says, if we see one of our fellow Christians entangled in a sin, we should try to help him free himself from it, but do it 'gently' and in love.

The Greek word used here, which has been translated as 'restore', meant to 'mend' or 'repair', as in setting bones after they were broken or mending torn fishing nets, or resolving disagreements between two parties.

Paul then warns us to be careful not to be swayed by the sinner. How often do we see people get pulled into things by their friends. Especially young people who think they can help one of their friends by trying to be a good influence on them, only to get caught up in their activities themselves because it looks harmless.

Help each other with burdens. This was the central theme of Christ's teachings. Here Paul is speaking of moral burdens and weaknesses. If we know someone is prone to being tempted by a certain sin, we should try to help them avoid the temptation and help strengthen this person's resolve by being there to support them.

Don't think you're capable of handling everything on your own. We are all weak when it comes to sin, and we all are tempted. Don't be too proud to ask your fellow Christians for help.

If you think you can handle everything by yourself, then you're deceiving yourself.

So Paul tells us to help each other and share our burdens.

Read Galatians 6:4-10

This seems contradictory to the previous verse. Now Paul seems to be telling us NOT to depend on others where before he tells us to depend on others.

This is an example where things can get lost in the translation. What Paul is actually saying here is, although we need to depend on others to HELP us AVOID sin, AFTER we have sinned, we need to take responsibility for it ourselves and not blame anyone else for those actions. Take personal responsibility for yourself and your actions. On judgment day, there will be no one else standing there with you to help relieve you of your guilt. Only YOU will give an account to God for your actions, and only YOU will be judged for them.

Now Paul slips in a little "But wait a minute—don't forget me." He asked the Galatians to not take for granted the teachers who instruct them in the Word of God and reminds them that those teachers needed to be compensated for their time and effort. We get a little insight to Paul's thinking here by reading what he wrote to the Philippians.

Read Philippians 4:14-16

Paul goes on to say the gifts were appreciated and God would reward them for their support. But what we learn from this is that the Philippians were the only ones giving Paul financial support.

But Paul doesn't let this fleeting thought get him sidetracked. In verse 7, he quickly continues with the point he is trying to make. "A man reaps what he sows."

This is one of the Biblical verses that has become widely used. We've heard it over and over, and many people don't even realize it is from the Bible. First, Paul uses this 'saying' as a negative thing. If you sin, you will reap destruction.

But then Paul says if you do things to please God, you will reap eternal life. So this applies not only negatively, but also positively. Sow bad things, reap bad things. Sow good things, reap good things. This was the basis for my aunt's favorite quote, "What goes around comes around."

In Verse 8, we see Paul changing his focus. Until now, he has been talking about inheriting 'the kingdom of God', but now he has switched to obtaining 'eternal life'. The first is focused on the inheritance (just as Israel inherited the promised land), the second is focused on the blessed life that will be enjoyed because of this inheritance. It's one thing to inherit something, it's something else to consider how the inheritance will affect us.

He continues this train of thought by prompting them to continue doing good, even though at times it might seem tiresome and seem it's getting them nowhere. How often do we feel like the good guy finishes last. It's always the good ones who get trampled and taken advantage of. But Paul says it might seem that way now, but don't give up because you WILL reap the harvest eventually. Of course, he's speaking of our reward in Heaven.

Take every opportunity to do good for others, especially fellow believers. When Paul says this, he is not saying NOT to do good for non-believers, but 'family comes first'. Fellow believers are a part of your family because we are all brothers and sisters in Christ, and therefore, they should come first.

Another verse that makes this idea of family first is 1 Timothy 5:8: *"Anyone who does not provide for their relatives, and especially for their own household, has denied the faith and is worse than an unbeliever."*

Read Galatians 6:11-13

Up to this point, this letter had probably been dictated by Paul to a scribe. But now Paul takes the pen himself and finishes the letter in his own hand. He may have been writing large for emphasis, or it may have been because of his poor eyesight. Either way, the point he was making here was that he is writing this next part himself.

Paul reverts back to his original reason for writing this letter. The Judaizers are preaching to the Galatians they must be circumcised. He says the ONLY reason they are doing this is to save their own skin. By advocating circumcision, the Jews who were against Christianity would be less likely to persecute them. They would accept them.

Also, Paul says by believing in the 'law', these Judaizers can ease their own guilt for persecuting and killing Christ. Even the Judaizers and the other Jews who have been circumcised don't obey all of the law, but if they can convince the Christians to be circumcised, then they can point fingers at them and say 'see, even the Christians believe the law can save them.

Read Galatians 6:14-18

Paul expresses his desire to be faithful. He says, "may I never accept anything other than the power of the cross of Jesus." When he says "the world has been crucified to me and I to the world," the word translated as 'world' here means 'everything that is against God'.

He is claiming his complete separation from anything unGodly.

Whether you are circumcised or not doesn't matter. The only thing that matters is you become a new creation. When you come to Christ, you undergo a transformation resulting in an entirely new being.

Read 2 Corinthians 5:17

Only those who truly believe this and follow this rule will obtain peace and mercy from God, even God's chosen people (Greek words used here literally translates to 'people of Israel').

Paul's meaning here is that the believing Jews and Gentiles ARE God's chosen people because they are the new seed of Abraham and the heir according to the promise. In ancient times, the Greek word for 'marks' was used when talking about a 'brand' that was placed on slaves and animals to identify their owners. Paul is saying he has been 'branded' as belonging to Christ.

He may have been speaking figuratively here, however he may have meant the stoning, the beatings, and his 'illness' (possibly his blindness) that he has suffered in becoming a follower of Christ have left physical scars, marking him as a 'servant of Christ'.

He closes with a blessing toward them, wishing them God's grace, and once again calling them his brothers and sisters, letting them know his love for them.

Lord, help us to show others we are a new creation as we live our lives day to day. Amen.

F.A.C.T.S.

The Letters to

THE CORINTHIANS

Paul Of Tarsus

So far in our study of Paul, he has been on two of his missionary journeys. He's been to Corinth, Thessalonica, and to Galatia and established churches all over the region.

We've studied his letters to Thessalonica and to Galatia. Soon after writing the letter of Galatians, about 53 AD, he began his third missionary journey. This journey involved a long ministry at Ephesus, a major port city on the western coast of Asia Minor with a harbor on the shores of the Aegean Sea. It was a center of trade from the sea and the hub of the region's road system, therefore, it was a thriving city. It was an administrative center for the Romans, had religious shrines, a spacious theater, a stadium, and many elegant public buildings, giving Ephesus an integral place in the cultural life of the entire region.

Paul worked for over two years at Ephesus, probably making tents again, since we see in Acts 18:24-28 that Aquila and Priscilla were in Ephesus. This was the same tent maker Paul had worked for previously in Corinth. While living and working there, he taught the Gospel and his teachings were accepted by disciples of John the Baptist.

Read Acts 19:1-7

But some from the Jewish synagogue rejected what he was teaching and others wrongly believed the ability to heal was magic. So Paul had to contend with a lot of different mixed religious beliefs.

Read Acts 19:13-20

NOTE: a drachma was a silver coin that was worth a day's wages. Today if someone makes $10/hr., their day's wages would be $80 (so this is what a drachma would be worth today). So 50,000 of these would equal $4,500,000!

Artemis was the patron goddess of Ephesus. Some of the silversmiths who made silver shrines of the goddess became angry at the success of Paul's preaching. They were afraid this new Christian faith he was teaching would diminish the widespread reverence for the goddess and this would cause a loss of income for them.

The temple of Artemis at Ephesus was regarded as one of the seven wonders of the ancient world. It stood outside the city and attracted visitors from all over the region. Artemus and her brother, Apollo, were said to be the children of Zeus and Leto. Artemis was also known as the virgin huntress, fearless in opposing her adversaries. She was believed to be a mother goddess, a provider of fertility, and an overseer of children.

The theater at Ephesus could seat 24,000 people for plays, music, and religious ceremonies. It was also used for public meetings to discuss issues, approve actions of the city council, and announce new laws. There was a demonstration against Paul held in this theater, but a city clerk was able to convince the crowd to disperse without incident.

Read Acts 19:23-41

It was during the time he was in Ephesus that Paul wrote 1Corinthians, sometime between 54 and 56 AD.

1 Corinthians – Chapter 1

Paul stayed in Corinth about a year and a half in about 52-53 AD and founded one of his greatest churches there. This letter was written about 3 years later while he was in Ephesus, about 200 miles east and across the Aegean Sea from Corinth. Leaders of the Corinthian church had been sent to Ephesus to consult with Paul about some serious problems that had arisen in the church. This letter was written about 57 AD in answer to their visit. We know he wrote it before Pentecost (because of verse 16:8) and that he was planning a visit to Corinth (16:5-8), which he did visit according to Acts 20:2-3.

When Paul wrote this letter, there were no churches or buildings for Christians to meet together. Other than the temple in Jerusalem, the building of churches did not begin until 200 years later. Christians met in homes, halls, or wherever they could. There were a large number of Christians in Corinth—not one great congregation, but rather many small groups, each with its own leadership. The Greeks had a fondness for intellectual speculation and enjoyed interjecting their philosophic interpretations of Christianity. Rather than cooperating with each other for the good of Christ, they began separating into factions of different ideas and beliefs.

When Paul heard about the divisions within the church groups, as well as other problems such as jealousy, sexual immorality, and failure to discipline members, this letter was his way of addressing the situation.

Read 1 Corinthians 1:1-3

Paul begins by introducing himself and Sosthenes, who was well known by those in Corinth. Paul may have felt his letter would carry more weight if he included Sosthenes in the introduction, or Sosthenes may have been writing the letter as Paul dictated it. Sosthenes may have been one of the church leaders sent to consult with Paul.

Paul addresses the letter to the Christians in Corinth, those sanctified in Christ Jesus. Sanctified means chosen or set apart by Christ for His service. Then Paul adds that this letter is intended for everyone who has accepted Jesus as Lord and Savior, making it clear this is not a private letter. He recognizes other congregations may have the same issues as the Corinthian ones.

Paul includes in his greeting a reminder of God's gift of grace which brings peace to those who accept it.

Read 1 Corinthians 1:4-6

Paul was gentle when admonishing people. He knew how to ease into his purpose for writing by starting with a positive note. When we must correct others, it helps if we affirm what has already been accomplished in them. Paul affirms their strengths as Christians by reminding them of the spiritual gifts of knowledge and understanding God has bestowed on them.

Read 1 Corinthians 1:7-9

Although the Corinthian church members had all the spiritual gifts necessary to live a Christian life, witness for

Christ, and stand against the paganism and immorality in the bustling city of Corinth, they were instead using what God had given them to argue over which of their gifts was most important. Paul addresses this problem later in this letter.

Paul guarantees the believers they will be considered "blameless" when Christ returns, not because of their great gifts or their shining performance, but because Christ is faithful to His promise that all who accept Him will be saved from condemnation.

Read 1 Corinthians 1:10-12

The Greek word for *brothers and sisters (adelphoi)* refers here to believers, both men and women, as part of God's family. Believers share a unity that runs even deeper than that of blood brothers and sisters. Paul realizes not everyone can be in complete agreement on everything all the time. Any group of people will not agree on every issue, but there's a difference between having opposing viewpoints and being divisive. Harmony can exist if everyone focuses on the truly important matters—Jesus Christ is Lord. Petty differences should never divide Christians.

Because there was not yet a New Testament, Christian churches relied heavily on preaching and teaching for spiritual insight and meaning of the Old Testament. Some followed Paul, others followed Peter (Cephas), and still others followed Apollos, who was a popular preacher with a dynamic ministry in Corinth. Although all three of these men were united in their message, they had different personalities and ways of preaching and leading. By mentioning Jesus Christ ten times within the first ten verses, Paul makes it clear where the emphasis should be. God's message is more important than any human message.

Read 1 Corinthians 1:13-17

Paul is not diminishing the importance of baptism, but is stressing that his gift is preaching. He wanted his listeners to be impressed with his message, not his style. You don't have to be a great orator to share the gospel effectively. The power is in the story, not the storyteller. There is no place for pride or a know-it-all attitude within the church.

Read 1 Corinthians 1:18-20

Paul quotes from the Old Testament scripture found in Isaiah 29:14 to emphasize a point Jesus made many times; God's way of thinking is not the same as normal human wisdom. We can spend a lifetime accumulating human wisdom, but yet never learn how to have a personal relationship with God.

Read 1 Corinthians 1:20-25

Jews expected the Messiah to come as a conquering king who would restore the throne of David, accompanied by signs and miracles. Society, then and now, worships power, influence, and wealth. Jesus came as a poor and humble servant and offers His kingdom to those who have faith, not to those who do good deeds to earn His gifts. This looks foolish to the world. Many Jews considered the Good News of Jesus Christ to be foolishness, especially since he was crucified as a criminal. How could a criminal be a savior?

Many Greeks also considered the gospel as foolish. To them, no reputable person would be crucified because death was defeat, not victory. But Christ did not stay dead. His resurrection demonstrated His power over death.

Christ is our power, the only way to salvation. Knowing Christ personally is the greatest wisdom anyone can have. Paul, being a bit facetious, says the "foolish" people who simply accept Christ's offer of eternal life are actually the wisest of all, for they alone will live eternally with God.

Read 1 Corinthians 1:26-31

Salvation comes only through God's grace and the gift of His Son. Christ came to earth to show us righteousness and holiness, and to redeem us. When He ascended into heaven, He gave us the Holy Spirit to guide us. In this way, we have received God's wisdom. The way to salvation is so simple that any person who wants to can understand it, but the world tries to make it complicated. Salvation is totally from God through Jesus Christ. There is absolutely nothing we can do to earn our way into heaven. That is why Paul quotes scripture from Jeremiah 9:24 (maybe not a word for word quote, but the general gist of the verse).

No one should be boastful about his or her salvation, but give God the glory for His precious gift.

1 Corinthians – Chapter 2

Corinth was close to Athens, where the atmosphere was dominated by egotists who paraded themselves as philosophers. The attitude of Athens had penetrated the Church in Corinth.

Paul was a university man and outstanding scholar of his generation, but he despised show-offs who debated to impress others of their knowledge. True learning and true scholarship should make us humble and more broadminded.

Read 1 Corinthians 2:1

Paul is referring to his first visit to Corinth during his second missionary journey in AD 51 when he founded the church there as told about in Acts 18.

Read 1 Corinthians 2:2-5

Paul was a brilliant scholar who could have overwhelmed them with his human knowledge and intellectual influences, but he chose to humble himself and speak to them simply about the gospel of Jesus Christ, allowing the Holy Spirit to guide his words. We should follow Paul's example and keep our message simple and basic when telling others about Christ. When we try to analyze and show our knowledge of scripture by trying to explain it through scientific proof, we dilute the message. Allow the Holy Spirit to give power to your words by not complicating it with your vast human knowledge.

Paul is not denying the importance of studying the scripture in preparation for preaching and teaching. He was thoroughly educated in the scriptures. Effective preaching and teaching must be founded in knowledge of scripture combined with guidance of the Holy Spirit. However, Paul is warning about becoming puffed up in our own importance and showing off our knowledge. Keep the focus on Jesus, giving Him the glory.

Read 1 Corinthians 2:6-7

God's previously hidden wisdom and mystery has been revealed to us in the form of salvation through Jesus Christ. When Jesus rose from the dead, God's plan became crystal clear. His resurrection proved He had power over sin and death. Yet this plan remains a mystery to unbelievers because they simply refuse to accept it, choose to ignore it, or haven't yet heard about it.

Read 1 Corinthians 2:8

The rulers in Palestine—the high priest, King Herod, Pilate, the Pharisees, and the Sadducees—all rejected Jesus and put Him to death because they misunderstood Him. This rejection was predicted in Isaiah 53:3 and Zechariah 12:10-11. Paul continues by quoting scripture from Isaiah 64:4.

Read 1 Corinthians 2:9

It is beyond our comprehension to imagine what God has in store for us! "No human mind has conceived the things God has prepared for those who love Him!" Isaiah 65:17 and Revelation 21:1 tell us about a new heaven and new earth where we will live with Him forever. This gives us hope and courage to face the hardships of this life and to avoid being drawn into temptation. This world is not all there is—the best is yet to come!

Read 1 Corinthians 2:10-12

Believers can know the truth of God's plan through the wisdom of the Holy Spirit. Be still and listen. The Holy Spirit is the Spirit of God. No one knows what you are thinking except your own spirit. You alone know your deepest inner thoughts. It is the same with God. Only His Spirit can know what He is thinking. When Christ ascended into heaven, he left us the Holy Spirit to be our guide. If we will allow the Spirit to guide us, He will reveal to us what we need to know inasmuch as we can understand it. Our immature human minds cannot perceive all the truths of heaven, but we can rest assured through our faith we can know all we need to know to live this life on earth in our journey to heaven. The Holy Spirit is our GPS on our road to heaven. Listen to Him, and you won't be lost.

Read 1 Corinthians 2:13

Paul explains he is not writing his own personal views or impression of what God had revealed to him. He gives credit to the Holy Spirit for revealing the thoughts and words of God to him.

Read 1 Corinthians 2:14

Those who reject the knowledge of Christ, no matter how much earthly knowledge or worldly wise they are, cannot begin to grasp the mysteries of God. The idea of the Holy Spirit living within Christians seems silly and ridiculous to non-believers. They are deaf to His voice. Their line of communication to God isn't connected. They cannot hear, and therefore cannot understand His message.

Read 1 Corinthians 2:15-16

No one can understand all the things of God, but through the guidance of the Holy Spirit believers have some insight into God's thoughts and plans as He chooses to reveal to us according to our ability to understand. Through our earthly experiences, our minds are able to grasp specific truths others may not be able to comprehend because they have not experienced anything to give them that insight. Everyone we meet and everything we experience, good and bad, opens our minds and level of understanding.

Through the Holy Spirit, we "have the mind of Christ." We can talk with Him and expect his answers to our prayers. But in order to do so, we need to spend time in His presence and in His Word forming an intimate relationship with Him. When you pray, be still and listen—often.

1 Corinthians – Chapter 3

Read 1 Corinthians 3:1-3

When we are 'born again' we become babes in Christ. We must learn and grow to mature. We cannot immediately understand all of God's truths simply because we've accepted Christ. The people of the church of Corinth were acting like small children, quarrelling and allowing their differences to distract them from their worship. Immature Christians are still worldly, being controlled by their own desires.

Being controlled by your own desires stunts your growth in the Lord. Your goal should be to allow God's desires to become your own.

Read 1 Corinthians 3:4-6

Paul returns to the theme he began in chapter 1. He had no tolerance for hero worship of those who had taught them the gospel. The people were dividing themselves into separate belief systems according to the leader they wanted to follow: Peter, who had walked and talked with Christ on earth; Apollos, with his sophisticated, cultivated style; Paul, the famous missionary; and Christ himself.

Each leader has a particular job to perform. Paul planted the seed by interpreting spiritual truths and conveying the gospel to the people. Apollos was to nurture the seed by continuing the job in Paul's absence. As with flowers, we water them, but it is God who makes them grow.

The Corinthian believers began pledging their loyalty to different teachers. We should respect our church leaders, but never place them on pedestals that create barriers between people.

Read 1 Corinthians 3:7-9

Paul reminds them again not to worship any human worker for they all belong to God, and God alone is to be worshipped.

Read 1 Corinthians 3:10-11

Paul founded the church in Corinth. He taught the gospel of Christ, laying the foundation. Apollos was to continue the leadership of the church by helping the members understand and grow stronger in their faith. His purpose was to build on the foundation Paul left behind. A building is only as solid as its foundation. The foundation of the church, and all believers, is Jesus Christ. Paul warns leaders of the church to build with care, using high-quality materials that meet God's standards. These high-quality materials would be the right doctrine and sound teachings.

Read 1 Corinthians 3:12-15

On Judgment Day, Christ will be the judge who will separate the good builders from the bad. He will evaluate the church leaders to determine the sincerity of each person's work and whether they have been faithful to Jesus' instructions. Good workers will be rewarded;

unfaithful workers will be revealed as such. However, notice they will still be saved. They will be like someone barely escaping a burning building. All their possessions will be lost. All their accomplishments will be discarded.

Read 1 Corinthians 3:16-17

Just as our bodies are the temple of the Holy Spirit, the church is God's temple—not the building, but the assembly of members. It is not to be destroyed or ruined by controversy or divisions as members come together to worship God.

Read 1 Corinthians 3:18-19

"He catches the wise in their craftiness"; (This quote is taken from Job 5:13)

Paul is suggesting they cast off worldly wisdom, which causes them to evaluate their leaders by how well they present the message rather than the content of the message.

Read 1 Corinthians 3:20-23

"The Lord knows that the thoughts of the wise are futile." (This quote is taken from Psalm 94:11)

(Cephas is another name for Peter)

Nonbelievers are victims of life, always wondering if there is meaning to it. Believers understand the true purpose of life and can therefore use their life for that purpose. Nonbelievers fear death, but believers know Christ has conquered death, leaving nothing to fear. Believers know death is the beginning of eternal life with God.

1 Corinthians – Chapter 4

In this section of Paul's letter, he reprimands those he'd left in charge of leading the church for their arrogance and discontent and warns them what will happen when he returns to them.

Read 1 Corinthians 4:1-2

Paul urges his readers to think of "us" as servants of Christ delivering "the secret things of God." We've learned in the previous chapters the "us" he refers to is himself, Peter, and Apollos. The "secret things of God" is referring to the Gospel, the plan of salvation through Jesus Christ.

Apollos was a self-confident and strong leader who had been to Corinth and become a very effective leader in the church there. However, because he had made such a strong impact on them, the church members were split in their loyalties. Some felt they should be followers of Paul, and others thought they should become followers of Apollos.

When Paul wrote this letter, Apollos was probably with him. Paul wanted Apollos to return to Corinth, but he refused because this division of the church was too troubling to him. He did not want to encourage more of it.

So Paul wrote this letter rather than send Apollos with the message.

Paul goes on to explain how those entrusted with God's message are required to prove themselves faithful. As a servant of God, we must do what He tells us to do through the scripture and through the Holy Spirit. Each day, we are faced with opportunities to make choices, challenging us to do what we know is right.

Read 1 Corinthians 4:3-5

It is tempting for us to judge other Christians for the way they do, or do not, follow Christ. But only God knows their heart and their true intentions. He is the only one with the right to judge. When you judge, you consider yourself better than the person you are judging, and that is arrogant.

Paul reminds them of the Day of Judgment that is to come, when God will reveal those things hidden in our hearts and expose us for who we truly are. Those who are worthy will receive their praise from God.

Read 1 Corinthians 4:6-7

When we have respect for a leader, it is natural for us to feel loyalty toward them. Paul warns us not to allow these loyalties to cause divisions within the church. Our loyalty should be to Christ, not to His human servants. True spiritual leaders are representatives of Christ and have nothing to offer other than what God has given them. Those who spend more time debating church leadership rather than delivering Christ's message do not have Christ as their top priority.

Read 1 Corinthians 4:8-13

Paul pours out his anguish in a tirade of sarcasm. At his own expense, Paul had suffered through 18 months of his life setting up the church in Corinth, at great risk to his life. Soon after he left, the church members became rebellious and initiated personal attacks against him. Throughout this letter, Paul's moods bounce from anger to shame to sorrow to indignation.

Read 1 Corinthians 4:14-15

Although he had been hurt by their disloyalty to him, Paul lets them know how he still loves them as a father loves his children even when they disappoint him.

During this time in history, a "guardian" was a slave assigned as a special tutor and caretaker of a child. Paul is telling them he is more than their guardian, but more like a father. Because he was the founder of the church, he could be trusted to have its best interest at heart. His tough and harsh words were motivated by his love for them much like a father for his children.

Read 1 Corinthians 4:16

"Therefore I urge you to imitate me."

Paul didn't expect them to imitate him in everything he did, right or wrong. He was referring to his teachings. He'd taught them to walk close to God, to spend time in prayer and in the scriptures, to be aware at all times of God's presence in their lives, and to follow in the footsteps of Christ. This was Paul's basic message; a message we should not stray from no matter what our church leaders teach.

Read 1 Corinthians 4:17

Timothy was not literally Paul's son, but a young man Paul had been highly impressed with and allowed to join him on his second missionary journey. Timothy had helped Paul set up the early churches during their travels. Paul trusted Timothy to deliver his message and make sure his advice was received, read, understood, and implemented. We don't know if Timothy actually delivered this letter or if he was sent soon after the letter.

Read 1 Corinthians 4:18-21

It is not known for sure if Paul ever went back to Corinth, but it is likely he did. He speaks of a "painful visit" in 2 Corinthians, so it is thought he visited sometime between writing this letter and the second one and that it didn't go well.

Paul asks if he should come to them with a rod of discipline or with love and a spirit of gentleness. In this letter we see a little of both sides of Paul. He admonishes them, but with love and affection, just as a parent with a child.

We talk a lot about faith. We might know all the right words to say, but do our lives reflect God's power? Paul says the kingdom of God is to be *lived*, not merely discussed. There is a big difference between knowing the right words and living the right life. Allow God's power to work in your life by making the right choices in your daily activities. Let others see God's power in your life, not simply hear you talk about it.

1 Corinthians – Chapter 5

This chapter proves times don't change the way humans think and act. We are still weak in the same ways they were back then. Human nature and sin remains the same no matter what time period we live in. Paul has received a report about a church member who is having sexual relations with his step-mother.

Read 1 Corinthians 5:1-2

Rather than reprimand the man committing this sin, his fellow church members are congratulating him for his conquest. Paul is asking them why they are not mourning the wrong doing and why they haven't removed him from their fellowship.

Read 1 Corinthians 5:3-5

Paul tells them that although he is not with them physically, he is still a part of their congregation and is with them in spirit. As a member of their church, he asks them to carry out his wishes by removing the man from their fellowship.

The Greek word translated as *"flesh"* is *sarx,* which refers to the sinful state of human beings. So Paul tells them to point out his sinful exploits so he can understand the error of his ways and repent so his spirit may be saved. The man had fallen out of favor of the Lord by committing the sin. The only way he will know to repent is if they show him where he is wrong.

"Hand this man over to Satan" means to exclude him from the fellowship of the believers. When separated from the church, the man would be left alone with Satan, for Satan rules the world. Hopefully this reality would cause him to repent, destroying his sinful nature.

Although this action of removing immoral members from the church is necessary to keep them from corrupting others within the membership, we should do it in love the same as a parent disciplines a child to teach them. It should never be done out of anger or hatred, but to correct and restore the offender so he will be motivated to repent and return to the church.

Read 1 Corinthians 5:6-8

If the church members don't hold him accountable and continue to encourage him by congratulating him on his virile ploys, they are allowing his sin to penetrate the entire church. They need to keep their eyes on Christ and the sacrifice Christ made. Throw out the wickedness and hold fast to sincerity and truth.

Paul did not expect believers to be sinless. All of us struggle with sin on a daily basis. But he was referring to people who deliberately sin, feel no guilt, and refuse to repent. This kind of blatant sin, left uncorrected, can confuse and divide a congregation.

Yeast: As the Hebrews prepared for the exodus from Egypt, they were commanded to prepare unleavened bread because they did not have time to wait for the bread to rise. Since that time, yeast became a symbol for sin throughout the scriptures.

Read 1 Corinthians 5:9-11

Paul reminds them of a previous letter (now known as the lost letter because a copy was not preserved) in which he told them not to associate with immoral people, but they may have assumed he meant those outside the church. He tells them he was also referring to those within the church who were immoral.

The Greek word translated as *"brother or sister"* is *adelphos* and refers here to a believer, whether man or woman, as part of God's family.

The end of verse 10 says in order to not associate with people of this world who are immoral, greedy, swindlers, or idolaters, "In that case you would have to leave this world." We cannot disassociate ourselves from the world and still carry out the great commission of Christ. Jesus commanded us to go into the world and teach others about him and deliver the gospel to all. This would become impossible if we separate ourselves from unbelievers. But if we do not distance ourselves from those who claim to be Christians while living a life of sin, we hurt our testimony as well as diminish the message of Christ. A church is supposed to be the light of the world, God's light. But immoral members snuff out the light.

Read 1 Corinthians 5:12-13

The scriptures tell us not to judge others. However, Paul says we are not to judge those outside of the church. God will be their judge. But in order to help keep them on the right path, we must judge our fellow believers. If we discipline them and they still will not turn away from their immoral behavior, then it is our duty to expel them from the church fellowship. Paul quotes scripture from Deuteronomy including 13:5, 17:7, 19:19, 21:21, 22:21, 24, and 24:7. Each of these verses ends with *"You must purge the evil from among you."*

This chapter of verses give us instruction on dealing with open sin within a church congregation by a person who claims to be a Christian but sins without remorse. It does not give us permission to gossip or be critical of others. Nor should Paul's instructions be used for trivial matters, for revenge, or to settle individual problems between believers.

1 Corinthians – Chapter 6

Read 1 Corinthians 6:1

Paul is probably talking about disputes on property here, not criminal cases. Verse 7 indicates this by talking about being wronged or cheated. In ***Romans 13:3-4***, Paul says that authorities are there to punish wrong doers. So he distinguishes between disputes, which are to be handled among believers, and criminal wrong doing, which is to be handled by the authorities.

Paul is telling the Corinthians to take their property disputes to qualified Christians for settlement. In Paul's day the Romans allowed people to apply their own law in property matters. So taking these disputes to the authorities wouldn't do a lot of good.

Read 1 Corinthians 6:2

We, being the saints, shall reign with Christ and therefore have a hand in judging the worldly. Paul is saying Christians are fully capable to judge cases where believers have claims against each other because they view matters from a godly vantage point. When you compare our future role as judges of the world and of angels, judgments concerning things of this life are insignificant.

Read 1 Corinthians 6:3

We will judge angels. *Jude 6* tells us there are angels being held in 'dungeons' until the judgment day. These are the angels we will be judging along with Christ on that day.

Read 1 Corinthians 6:4

This could be interpreted one of two ways. Paul could be saying that even the least in the church are capable of judging such small matters better than a non-believer; or he could be sarcastically asking why a believer would allow a pagan judge to decide on a case when he is not qualified to decide on something that's between two Christians. Someone who is not a Christian would not see things in a godly way and therefore would make a decision based on material, rather than spiritual, motivation.

Read 1 Corinthians 6:5

Back in 1 Corinthians 4:14, Paul says he is not trying to shame them, but warn them because he loves them. But here Paul says, okay NOW I'm saying this to shame you! He asks them if they are all too stupid to settle a simple dispute between two Christians. He wants them to realize how ridiculous they are being.

Read 1 Corinthians 6:6

By choosing to go through the courts, this brings the dispute into the open for all to see. What kind of a witness are you as a Christian if you can't even work things out with one of your brothers or sisters in Christ? The world looks at this kind of behavior and sees the Christian as being no different from everyone else. Yet, we as Christians should be set apart from the things of this world so the world can see Christ shining through us. If we act the same as the rest of the world, we are destroying our testimony for Christ.

Read 1 Corinthians 6:7-8

Why does Paul say they are defeated if they have lawsuits among them? Their greed, retaliation and hatred prevents them from practicing unselfishness, forgiveness and love. This makes them act the same as the worldly, and therefore they are not set apart. Instead of allowing this to happen, a Christian attitude should make them feel they had rather be wronged or cheated than to act like this toward a brother or sister in Christ.

Read 1 Thessalonians 4:6

Read 1 Corinthians 6:9

In verse 8, Paul said that these Christians are acting in the wrong, bringing to mind wickedness. So in this verse he continues with this train of thought and asks if they realize the wicked will not go to heaven. He says don't be deceived into thinking these things are okay, because these things will prevent them from entering God's kingdom. He then goes on to describe the kinds of wickedness he's talking about.

Paul identifies three kinds of sexual immorality: adultery, male prostitution, and male homosexuality. Those who engage in such practices are explicitly excluded from God's kingdom.

Read 1 Corinthians 6:10

Also excluded from His kingdom will be thieves, those who are greedy, drunkards, slanderers and swindlers.

Read Revelations 21:8 & 22:14-15

Read 1 Corinthians 6:11

There is hope even for these people. God does save and sanctify people like those described. Paul says there were Christians among them who used to be as bad as those he had described, but they had been washed clean.

Read Ephesians 2:1-5

Read 1 Corinthians 6:12

Here Paul is probably quoting some in the Corinthian congregation who feel that because they are saved by grace, they can do whatever they want and still go to heaven. But Paul points out that although they have this 'freedom' from the law, they will still have to suffer the consequences of their actions and this sinful nature can cause problems, not only for them as a human being, but as a Christian. A Christian must also consider the good of others and be aware of the consequences he may inflict on others. One can become enslaved by those actions in which he 'freely' indulges.

Read 1 Corinthians 10:23

Read 1 Corinthians 6:13

Again Paul is quoting some Corinthians who were claiming that eating and digesting food is a physical act that has no bearing on one's inner spiritual life. Likewise, they were saying, the act of promiscuous sexual activity is also a physical act and does not affect one's spiritual life. But Paul says the human body was intended for the Lord.

Read Romans 12:1

We are to use our bodies to glorify the Lord and allow Christ to be seen through us. If we are doing immoral acts, we are preventing Christ from working through us. Paul is denying that what one does with his body is unimportant.

Read 1 Corinthians 6:14

Paul goes on to give an illustration as to how important the body is. God holds our bodies in such high regard that he saw fit to raise Christ's body from the grave and, eventually, the believer's body will also be resurrected.

See Romans 6:5

A body destined for resurrection should not be used for immorality.

Read 1 Corinthians 6:15

Read 1 Corinthians 12:27

Read Romans 12:5

It is not just the spirit that is a member of Christ's body. It's the whole person, consisting of spirit and body. This fact gives dignity to the human body. Would you present a member of Christ to a prostitute? Of course not!

The prostitutes of Corinth were dedicated to the service of Aphrodite, the goddess of love and sex. (Aphrodite was the Greek name. The Romans referred to her as Venus.) She was the principal deity of Corinth and her temple was among the most magnificent buildings in the city. Kept there were a thousand priestesses (or public prostitutes) at public expense, always ready for immoral indulgence as worship to their goddess. Some of the Corinthian Christians, having been used to a religion that encouraged such immoral living, were finding it difficult to adapt to their new religion which prohibited immoral living.

Read 1 Corinthians 6:16

In a sexual relationship the two bodies become one, and a new human being may emerge from their union. The two will become one flesh is from Genesis 2:24 and is repeated in Matthew 19:5 & Ephesians 5:31. This refers to a man and his wife and sexual relations outside the marriage bond are a gross perversion of the divinely established marriage union.

Read 1 Corinthians 6:17

The believers spiritual union with Christ is a higher union than the bond of marriage between a man and a woman. It is the perfect model for the kind of unity that should mark a marriage relationship as described in Ephesians 5:21-33.

Read 1 Corinthians 6:18

Why should you flee? See verse 9 again. Verse 18 tells us why sexual perversion is so much worse than most other sins. All other sins man commits are outside of his body. But sexual acts actually occur on or within the body, gratifying one's physical self in a unique way that no other sin will or can.

Read 1 Corinthians 6:19

The body is the temple of the Holy Spirit, which dwells within you if you are a Christian. As a Christian, you should value your body as a sacred place where God dwells and realize that by the Spirit's presence and power, we can overcome temptation.

Read Romans 8:9

Read 1 Corinthians 6:20

Christ purchased your body with His blood when he was crucified for your sins. It now belongs to Him, not you. Therefore, you are to honor God with your body.

Read Colossians 3:17

In chapters 5 & 6, Paul has asked seven questions to emphasize seven very important principles:
1. Do you not know a little leaven leavens the whole lump?
2. Do you not know the saints will judge the earth?
3. Do you not know we are to judge angels?
4. Do you not know the unrighteous will not inherit the kingdom of God?
5. Do you not know your bodies are members of Christ?
6. Do you not know he who joins himself to a prostitute becomes one body with her?
7. Do you not know your body is a temple of the Holy Spirit?

If we know these seven principles, how should it affect our behavior as Christians?

1 Corinthians – Chapter 7

This chapter is a good example why we should study the Bible in depth rather than take verses out of context. There are several instances when Paul gives his opinion based on the situation during that era of time. If you take those verses out of context, you might believe he is giving instruction from God when he is merely expressing his opinion. If you read carefully, he clearly tells when the directive is from God and when it is Paul's own opinion.

In verse 26, Paul refers to the present crisis. Corinth was over-run with immorality and corruption. This is what Paul is referring to in his letter. While looking around at what was going on, the Corinthians wrote to Paul asking him several questions, obviously one of which concerned marriage. This chapter is written in response to their question.

Read 1 Corinthians 7:1-2

Paul is NOT suggesting it is good for man not to marry, but is referring to a quote from their letter questioning this idea. He tells them when surrounded by the kind of immoral corruption taking place in Corinth during this period of time, he is strongly in favor of marriage. By having their own wife, or own husband, they won't be as tempted by the prostitutes and immorality surrounding them.

Read 1 Corinthians 7:3-5

Married couples should have normal sexual relations. Abstinence deprives the other partner of his or her natural right and may cause temptation.

Read 1 Corinthians 7:6

Here Paul makes it clear this is his advice, not a command from God. Although Paul is says it's a good idea to marry and for husbands and wives to keep each other sexually content, it is not mandatory.

Read 1 Corinthians 7:7-9

Paul says he wishes all men were like him, unmarried. Paul feels it is a gift from God he has no desire to marry. But he says men who cannot control their sexual desires should get married so they won't be tempted to live immorally.

Read 1 Corinthians 7:10

Paul is teaching something Jesus taught during His earthly ministry— a married woman must not separate from her husband. He makes it clear this is a command from God.

Paul did not hear Jesus preach this, but may have heard it from other disciples or from a special revelation from Jesus or the Holy Spirit.

Read 1 Corinthians 7:11

If a woman does leave her husband, she must remain unmarried or be reconciled with her husband. In other words, married couples should stay together.

Read 1 Corinthians 7:12-13

Here Paul makes it clear this next statement is his opinion, not a command from the Lord. He says, in his opinion, having a spouse who is not a believer is NOT grounds for divorce—unless the non-believer refuses to stay with the believer.

Read 1 Corinthians 7:14

Paul expounds on his logic. The unbelieving partner is influenced by the Godly life of the Christian partner. Through the Christian partner, the Holy Spirit becomes influential in the family. The children have the advantage of being under the influence of at least one Christian parent.

Read 1 Corinthians 7:15

But if the unbeliever wants to leave, let him/her go. The Christian is not obligated to remain married to someone who doesn't want to be with them. God has called us to live in peace, and if the unbeliever—who doesn't want to be there—is forced to remain with the Christian, there will be no peace in their home.

Read 1 Corinthians 7:16

By not leaving, the Christian partner may have the opportunity to bring the unbeliever to Christ.

Read 1 Corinthians 7:17-19

No matter what economic, social, or religious station in life God has seen fit to place you, each Christian is to live contentedly for the Lord. What matters is we keep God's commands. Paul addresses the issue of that day, which was whether circumcision is necessary to be a Christian. He reminds them it is not important whether one is circumcised or not.

Read 1 Corinthians 7:20-21

Whatever your status when you were called by God to become a Christian, you should be content in it. If you were married, stay married, even if your spouse is an unbeliever. If you were a slave, don't allow that to dampen your enthusiasm as a Christian—but if you can gain your freedom, do it. He's not asking us not to grow in life, only to be content and joyful no matter what our situation. There is nothing wrong with seeking to improve your condition, but be content in every stage.

Read 1 Corinthians 7:22-24

Being in Christ frees us from earthly bonds and bounds us to be workers for Christ. Christ has purchased us with His blood and therefore, our focus should be on Him and not man. Whatever situation you are in, God has a purpose for you being there.

Read 1 Corinthians 7:25

Paul moves on to the Corinthians' next question, which pertains to virgins or unmarried women. He makes it clear again that this is his opinion and not a command from God. But he is not denying he is writing under divine inspiration. In fact, in verse 40 he says he believes the Spirit of God is influencing him in his answers to their questions.

Read 1 Corinthians 7:26

"Present crisis" is a reference to the pressures a Christian faced at that time of immoral and particularly hostile environment. Paul's recommendations here do not apply to all times and all situations. He is addressing their current situation only.

Read 1 Corinthians 7:27-28

Paul tells them to stay as they are. Don't seek a divorce if you are married. If you are unmarried, then stay that way if you can without being tempted. But if you feel the need to be married in order to avoid temptation, then you will not be sinning.

By being married, they will be facing extra hardships as Christians. The 'present crisis' included a great deal of persecution toward Christians. It's easier to suffer and be persecuted for Christ when you only need to be concerned about yourself. But if you're married, then you have to be concerned for your mate and their well-being. It's more difficult to watch someone you love be persecuted.

Read 1 Corinthians 7:29-31

This appears to contradict Paul's previous statements if you take them out of context. Paul is simply pointing out how fleeting our earthly life is. The time for doing the Lord's work is short. Don't be unduly concerned with the things of this world because material things are changing and disappearing. What Paul is saying here is not to count on these things. Don't count on the fact that you're married because tomorrow your circumstances may change. Don't revel in your present happiness, because it can change in an instant. Be prepared for those changes by not depending on your circumstances. Lean on the Lord and live for doing His work.

In the following verses, Paul goes on to explain those statements which seem contradictory. If you continue to read and not take those verses out of context, his point becomes more clear.

Read 1 Corinthians 7:32-35

An unmarried man or woman can concentrate more on pleasing God, but a married man or woman must be concerned about pleasing their mates. So it is better to remain unmarried so you can live your life more fully for the Lord, giving all your attention and devotion to Him. This is particularly true during times of persecution.

Read 1 Corinthians 7:36-38

Whether you marry or not, it's okay. God does not fault you for wanting to be married or not wanting to be married. Paul is only saying it's easier to live your life more fully for the Lord if you are not married.

Read 1 Corinthians 7:39-40

If a woman's husband dies, it is okay for her to remarry. However, Paul sticks to his belief that she could be happier putting all her efforts into serving the Lord rather than marrying again.

1 Corinthians – Chapter 8

One of the questions the Corinthians asked Paul in their letter concerned the eating of meat. There were many gods in Greece, and much of the meat offered for sale in public market places had first been offered in sacrifice to some idol. The question at issue involved not only the eating of the meat, but the matter of participating in social functions of their heathen friends, many of which functions were often accompanied with shameful acts.

Read 1 Corinthians 8:1-3

Look at verse 2—what a confusing verse! Some earlier manuscripts and ancient writings show this verse to say *"Those who think they have knowledge do not yet know as they ought to know. But whoever loves truly knows."*

Still confusing. Paul's point, however, is knowledge causes us to be filled with false pride. I believe what he is saying here is to not be arrogant about our knowledge in Christ, but to show all men love and compassion. Don't be judgmental, but loving. Paul is saying even the wisest and most knowledgeable Christians realize their knowledge is limited. God is the only one who knows all.

1 John 4:7-8 says *"Dear friends, let us love one another, for love comes from God. Everyone who loves has been born of God and knows God. Whoever does not love does not know God, because God is love."*

Read 1 Corinthians 8:4-6

Idols are man-made and have no power. The so-called 'gods' are from men's imaginations, not real gods. Yet, there are demons behind them.

Read Psalm 115:4-8

Read 1 Corinthians 10:20

In verse 5, Paul is saying there are many 'gods' and 'lords' people have come to believe in. He's not saying they exist, but there are a lot of beliefs among the people.

God the Father is the ultimate source of all creation. God the Son is the dynamic one through whom all things came into existence.

Read John 1:1-3

Read Colossians 1:15-16

Read 1 Corinthians 8:7-8

Some still want to believe the idols are gods and have powers. Christians who conceive of an idol as being real have a difficult time ridding themselves of this idea. So they think in eating meat that has been sacrificed to these idols they have involved themselves in the worship of them. But Paul says the food is no different from any other food. It's been slaughtered and ready to eat. Eating it won't bring us closer to God, nor will it make us any better or worse in His sight. Frankly, God doesn't care one way or the other if we eat the meat or not, as long as we are not doing it as an act of worship to the idol—or if we are not hurting our testimony as a Christian...

Read 1 Corinthians 8:9-13

Paul goes on to say even though we have the freedom of knowing it's okay with God, others may not understand this. He tells them even though they may have been invited into the idol's temples to feast on the meat, if they do so, they could hurt their testimony for Christ and cause others to turn away from Christ, therefore they would be sinning against Christ.

Paul says the weak Christian is influenced by the stronger one. If you do something that is perceived to be sinful, even though God accepts it, the weak brother may be appalled enough to withdraw from Christ.

It's also a sin against Christ because it breaks the unity of the members of the body (the church). Therefore, be careful not to do anything that will turn someone else against Christianity. There are a lot of believers and nonbelievers in this world who are looking for reasons to call Christians hypocrites, and all too often we give them plenty of reasons. A simple utterance of a naughty word, a purchase of a bottle of wine, a piece of gossip shared among friends, judging another person's past, or saying a blessing in public and then cursing during the meal—all of these seemingly innocent everyday occurrences can cause someone to turn away from wanting to be a Christian or cause a weak or new Christian from wanting to admit it.

Am I saying it is sinful to purchase a bottle of wine? Absolutely not. But it is an example of what Paul was talking about when discussing eating the meat from a sacrifice to an idol. It is not a sin against God, but it may cause someone who doesn't understand to question your sincerity as a Christian. That is why many Christians refuse to buy or drink alcohol. Not because it is a sin, but because they don't want to cause this type of misunderstanding.

When faced with decisions, weigh the influence your decision might have on those around you. We are not saved by our works or lack of sin, but by God's grace. With a Christian's freedom from law come Christian responsibilities to help strengthen other Christians and God's Kingdom here on earth.

1 Corinthians – Chapter 9

The people of Corinth questioned Paul's genuine apostleship. Now he defends himself as an apostle.

Read 1 Corinthians 9:1-3

Paul says he is free from the old law the same as any other Christian. To prove he is an apostle, he reminds them he has seen Jesus Christ. He was visited by the risen Christ on the road to Damascus. He reminds them they are the spiritual fruit of his apostleship. His ministry is what won them to Christ, so how could they deny he is an apostle?

Read 1 Corinthians 9:4

As an apostle, it is Paul's right to have the church supply his earthly needs. In Luke 10:7, Jesus said workers deserve their wages. *("Stay there, eating and drinking whatever they give you, for the worker deserves his wages...")* Paul echoes this thought and urges the church to pay their Christian workers. It is our duty to see those who serve us in the ministry (pastors, teachers, and other spiritual leaders) are fairly compensated.

Read 1 Corinthians 9:5-6

Here Paul is asserting his right to be married to one wife. This does not mean he was married, only that he felt he had the right to marry if he wanted, just as other apostles, such as Peter (A.K.A. Cephas), had done. According to what Paul is stating here, evidently both James and Jude (A.K.A. Judas), the brothers of Jesus, were married, and both of them had attained leadership status within the church in Jerusalem.

Read 1 Corinthians 9:7-11

Paul considers himself a servant and soldier for Christ and asks what soldier has to pay his own way? Doesn't the country for which he fights take care of him? Who would plant and harvest a vineyard and not enjoy the fruits of his labors? Paul is asking why he should continue to convert people to Christ and not have the pleasure of their friendship. Instead, they want to turn against him. He says even the old laws of Moses allowed for men to enjoy their harvest. Quoting the law found in Deuteronomy 25:4, he says "Do not muzzle an ox while it is treading out the grain." In other words, if the ox is doing his work, don't interfere by causing him grief. Let him enjoy his labors and he will produce more. Then Paul asks, do you think God was really concerned about oxen? Of course not! He was speaking of the witnesses for Him, those who were working His spiritual fields.

Sometimes we hear people complain about preachers and church workers not working outside the church to support themselves. People see them as "riding a gravy train" and having a cushy job. But here Paul sets forth the principle that Christian workers should be paid for their labors in material ways: food, lodging, and salary.

Read 1 Corinthians 9:12

Paul goes on to say that even though he had a right to the support of the church, he hadn't taken advantage of it because he didn't want to do anything to hinder the message of the Gospel. He didn't want anyone to view him as a free-loader. His love for the Corinthian people made him hesitate to make himself a burden to them. Yet, this was the very reason they became suspicious of him. They didn't understand why he wasn't asking for compensation since they were driven by their love of material possessions and greed.

Read 1 Corinthians 9:13-14

The Corinthian believers would have understood this illustration because of the practice in pagan temples in Greece and Rome, which were all around them. Whenever an animal was sacrificed, the meat was used to throw a feast for all the worshippers. Also, they had a vast knowledge of the Old Testament.

Read Leviticus 7:32-34

Read 1 Corinthians 9:15-16

Paul explains even though it was his right to claim these things, he is not asking for any of it. He does not want any payment for preaching the Gospel of Christ. He is proud of the fact he does it out of love and not for support of his fellow believers. He says he is compelled by his love of God and could not stop preaching the Gospel if he wanted to. It was a strong desire that motivated him to preach. It was not a burden.

Read 1 Corinthians 9:17-18

Paul explains that because he is choosing to preach voluntarily, without charging, he is rewarded by satisfaction of knowing he has done it for the Lord out of love and devotion. But if he were to do it involuntarily and charge for his services, he would not feel that kind of satisfaction.

When our focus is on living for Christ, our rights become comparatively unimportant.

Read 1 Corinthians 9:19-23

Paul committed himself to win as many souls as possible to the Lord. Therefore, his entire life was given to saving others. He changed his approach depending upon who he was trying to reach. He joined in their customs and obeyed their laws and rules so they would accept him among them. He gave up his own personal freedoms and rights and privileges so others would be more accepting of him. But when he was with the Gentiles (those without the law), then he acclimated himself into their culture, as long as it did not violate his allegiance to Christ. When he speaks of the weak, he is referring to those spiritually weak and could easily be led astray. He would abstain from certain practices so they would not see him as hypocritical. His only motive was to spread the gospel and share in the joy of bringing others the joy of salvation.

We find some examples of things he did in the book of Acts:

Acts 16:3 *"Paul wanted to take him* [Timothy] *along on the journey, so he circumcised him because of the Jews who lived in that area, for they all knew that his father was a Greek."*

Acts 18:18 *"Paul stayed on in Corinth for some time. Then he left the brothers and sisters and sailed for Syria, accompanied by Priscilla and Aquila. Before he sailed, he had his hair cut off at Cenchreae because of a vow he had taken."*

Acts 21:20-26 *"[20]When they heard this, they praised God. Then they said to Paul: "You see, brother, how many thousands of*

Jews have believed, and all of them are zealous for the law. ²¹They have been informed that you teach all the Jews who live among the Gentiles to turn away from Moses, telling them not to circumcise their children or live according to our customs. ²²What shall we do? They will certainly hear that you have come, ²³so do what we tell you. There are four men with us who have made a vow. ²⁴Take these men, join in their purification rites and pay their expenses, so that they can have their heads shaved. Then everyone will know there is no truth in these reports about you, but that you yourself are living in obedience to the law. ²⁵As for the Gentile believers, we have written to them our decision that they should abstain from food sacrificed to idols, from blood, from the meat of strangled animals and from sexual immorality." ²⁶The next day Paul took the men and purified himself along with them. Then he went to the temple to give notice of the date when the days of purification would end and the offering would be made for each of them."

Read 1 Corinthians 9:24-25

The Corinthians had the Isthmian games, which occurred every other year and were second only to the Olympic games in importance, so they were very familiar with foot races.

Winning a race requires purpose and discipline. The Christian life takes hard work and self-denial. The disciplines of prayer, Bible study, and worship gives us the stamina we need to run our race toward our heavenly reward.

The prize they received back then would be a perishable wreath, much like the ones the horses receive today when they win a race. Paul goes on to say these runners in their races receive a crown, or wreath, that won't last, it's perishable. But as Christians we are running the race to receive a crown that will last forever.

Read 2 Timothy 4:8

Read James 1:12

Read 1 Peter 5:4

Read 1 Corinthians 9:26-27

In keeping with the spirit of the games, Paul has switched to boxing. He is referring to the Christian life as a boxing match. He does not aimlessly beat the air, but disciplines his body in serving Christ. He says he keeps himself in check because he doesn't want to win all these souls to Christ and then find in the end he has been disqualified because of his own sinfulness.

Read Philippians 3:14

Although we are now into chapter 9 of his letter, Paul has remained true to his message.

Read 1 Corinthians 3:10-15

Paul emphasizes a life of strict discipline. Because of his commitment to winning souls to Christ, he kept himself free of material entanglements and anything else that might distract him from his goal. Freedom and discipline are important tools to be used in God's service.

Paul gives us several important principles for ministry:
1. Find common ground with those you contact;
2. Avoid a know-it-all attitude;
3. Make others feel accepted;
4. Be sensitive to their needs and concerns;
5. Look for opportunities to tell others about Christ.

Rather than be an observer of the race, or show up for one or two laps, train diligently—your spiritual growth depends on it.

1 Corinthians – Chapter 10

A lot of what happened in the Old Testament was symbolic of what was to come. To fully understand what Paul is explaining in this chapter, we must first look at some of the Old Testament.

Read Exodus 13:21-22

Read Exodus 14:29-31

Read Numbers 9:15-23

Read Numbers 14:14

Read Deuteronomy 1:32-33

In this chapter of 1 Corinthians, Paul recognizes much of the Old Testament is symbolic of what is to come and explains how it all ties together.

Read 1 Corinthians 10:1

As shown in the verses from the Old Testament shown above, the cloud was God's leadership and guidance. His guidance never failed them.

Read 1 Corinthians 10:2

As a people, they were united under God's redemptive program and they submitted to Moses as their deliverer and leader. The word 'baptized' is used to depict their submission to Moses, just as Christian baptism depicts the believer's submission to Christ as Lord and Savior.

Read 1 Corinthians 10:3-4

The spiritual food and drink (the manna and water) from the rock were symbolic of Christ (the rock), the bread and water of life. These represented the spiritual sustenance God continually provides for his people through Christ as we read in John 6:30-35:

So they asked him, "What sign then will you give that we may see it and believe you? What will you do? Our ancestors ate the manna in the wilderness; as it is written: 'He gave them bread from heaven to eat.' " Jesus said to them, "Very truly I tell you, it is not Moses who has given you the bread from heaven, but it is my Father who gives you the true bread from heaven. For the bread of God is the bread that comes down from heaven and gives life to the world." "Sir," they said, "always give us this bread." Then Jesus declared, "I am the bread of life. Whoever comes to me will never go hungry, and whoever believes in me will never be thirsty.

Read 1 Corinthians 10:5

In spite of the remarkable privileges God had given to Israel, they failed to obey Him, thus incurring His displeasure. Of all of the adults who came out of Egypt, only two were actually allowed to enter the promised land of Canaan, Caleb and Joshua as we read in Numbers.

Read Numbers 14:20-24; and 14:30

F.A.C.T.S.

Read 1 Corinthians 10:6-7

Here Paul is referring to the incident of the golden calf as described in Exodus.

Read Exodus 32:1-6

Read 1 Corinthians 10:8

Paul is referring to Israel's joining herself to Baal as told in Numbers.

Read Numbers 25:1-9

They participated in the worship of Baal and engaged in sexual immorality with the prostitutes. Although Paul quotes 23,000 as the number that died, in Numbers 25:9, we are told it was 24,000. Paul's purpose was not to be exact, but to make his point that A LOT of people died because of their wickedness. Writers at that time were not so concerned about being exact as they are today. They were simply trying to get their point across.

Read 1 Corinthians 10:9-10

Read Numbers 16:41-50

Read Exodus 12:23

Paul links the event of the plague, due to the grumbling of the Israelites, to the destroying angel of Exodus. His message is "Do not cross (or test) the Lord!"

Read 1 Corinthians 10:11

"culmination (or fulfillment) of the ages": This is the period of time between Christ's death and resurrection and continuing into the future until Christ's second coming and beyond. It is the period of fulfillment, when all that God has done for His people throughout all the ages comes to fruition in the Messiah.

Paul is explaining the importance of the Old Testament scriptures. He says these things are important for us to know so we can learn from the mistakes those people made. Let it warn us of what could happen.

We must learn from history. That is the purpose of studying history in school; so we can learn from previous mistakes. The Old Testament is Jewish history and has been preserved for us to read, study, and learn from the mistakes made so we don't repeat them.

Read Romans 15:4

The same temptations causing those delivered out of Egypt to be banned from the Promised Land were very much the same temptations the people of Corinth were facing, lustful indulgence.

Read 1 Corinthians 10:12-13

The Greek word for temptation or tempted can also mean testing or tested. Don't be over-confident or too sure you can withstand the temptations of this world. Keep your guard up. Temptation in itself is not a sin. Everyone is tempted, even Jesus (as told in Matthew 4:1-11). The sin is in yielding to that temptation, giving into it. God will not allow you to be tempted beyond what you can handle. Anytime there is temptation, He provides an alternative for us so we can choose the way out. He will give us the strength to resist if we will accept His help.

Read 1 Corinthians 10:14

The Corinthian Christians had come out of a background of paganism. As they went through their everyday lives, they were surrounded by temples for the worship of Apollo, Asclepius, Demeter, Aphrodite and other pagan gods and goddesses. The strongest temptation was probably that of Aphrodite with its many 'sacred prostitutes'.

Read 1 Corinthians 10:15-17

Paul says, 'okay, you're reasonable people, you should be able to grasp this'. Then he describes the Lord's Supper and how the loaf and the cup are symbols to remind us of Christ and His sacrifice. The Lord's Supper was instituted at the Jewish Passover before Christ was crucified (as told in Matthew 26:17-30; Mark 14:12-26; & Luke 22:7-23.)
"one loaf" : The act of many believers partaking of one loaf of bread symbolizes the unity of the body of Christ, the church, which is nourished by the one bread of life, Jesus.

Read 1 Corinthians 10:18-21

When those of the Old Testament sacrificed animals at God's altar and then ate the meat, they participated in the worship of God. Likewise, when the pagans eat the meat from their sacrifices, they are worshipping demons. The idols are not gods, but in reality, it was demons that were the objects of idol worship. Paul doesn't say it is wrong to eat the meat that has been sacrificed to idols, but it is wrong to eat it with the pagans as part of their worship for then they would be participants in worshiping the demons.

Read 1 Corinthians 10:22

Paul then warns them not to share in the pagan worship or they will arouse the Lord's jealousy.

Read Exodus 20:5

Read 1 Corinthians 10:23-24

Once again Paul is quoting the Corinthians who believed since they are not 'under the law', they have the freedom to do as they want without consequence. But he tells them to beware. Just because you have freedom from the law of Moses, your actions may not be beneficial to you or to others. There could be consequences. You must consider the good of others as well as yourself.

Read Galatians 6:2

Read 1 Corinthians 10:25-26

Paul quotes from Psalm 24:1 which is used at Jewish mealtimes as a blessing. So you may eat anything sold in the meat market, even if it was originally a sacrifice to an idol, because once it is in the public market it loses its pagan religious significance.

Read 1 Corinthians 10:27-30

If you are invited to a meal by an unbeliever and they place the meat in front of you, don't question if it's been sacrificed to idols or not. If the subject doesn't come up, then eat. But if you are told it was a sacrifice to an idol, then you must not eat it.

Paul has already said it's okay to eat meat sacrificed to idols once it is in the marketplace. So now why would he say not to eat it at a neighbor's table? Even worse than that, you can eat it even if you know it's been sacrificed, as long as the subject doesn't come up. How does that make sense?

Paul's reasoning here is the meat is okay to eat, but if the meat has been identified as meat sacrificed to idols and you eat it, the others at the table—whether believers or unbelievers—may think you condone (or even are willing) to participate in the worship of idols.

Paul says don't eat it, for the sake of the man who told you and "for conscience sake"—not for YOUR conscience, but the other man's conscience. You might cause the other man to think it is alright to eat meat sacrificed to idols, even though he might have had doubts about it before. So you will have unintentionally caused that man to falter. Or, if he was an unbeliever, he may think Christians worship both God and pagan idols. Our actions may not be sinful, but our intent, or the way others perceive our intent, is a different matter.

Then Paul asks, 'why should my freedoms, given to me by God's grace, be compromised because of what someone else might think?'

Read 1 Corinthians 10:31-33

Answering his own question, Paul says the reason is because we need to be sure God is glorified in everything we do, and not cause anyone around us to have reason to think ill of Christians or of God. Although what we do may not be sinful, it could be misinterpreted by others, causing them to stumble or stray away from the Truth of Jesus. Living to glorify God will result in doing what is beneficial for others, whether Christians or non-Christians. Paul is not saying he will compromise the truths of the gospel in order to please everyone, but he will consider his fellow man and not cause anyone to be offended by his daily life because if he offends someone, then he can't witness to them, and they won't receive the gospel and be saved.

Our purpose as Christians is to bring others to Jesus. We cannot do that if those we are trying to win do not respect us. If we are doing things others see as questionable, even if God doesn't, we could lose their respect and be seen as hypocrites. This is exactly what most nonbelievers are looking for so they can discredit Christianity. We need to make sure we do not give them more ammunition.

1 Corinthians – Chapter 11

This was a difficult chapter for me. I prayed and studied it, then prayed some more for guidance from the Holy Spirit. During a church service one Sunday morning, my eyes were opened. Whatever was hindering my understanding of this chapter seemed to lift, and I could suddenly see the meaning more clearly.

Read 1 Corinthians 11:1

Paul is not being boastful. Although not sinless, he was a living example of what a Christian should be. The gospels hadn't been written yet, so most of those in the church of Corinth didn't know much about Jesus. If he'd said to imitate Jesus, they wouldn't have understood. Paul had spent almost two years in Corinth and built a trusting relationship with many of the new believers. So he was the only example for them to follow.

Read 1 Corinthians 11:2-3

Paul's concern here is the proper relationship between men, women, Jesus, and God in regards to worship. Without our head, our body would be worthless. Man is to be helpful to Christ, working for and serving Him.

Without Christ, a man's life is worthless. Woman was created to be a help-mate for man. If married, she is to support and assist her husband. Does this mean she is worthless if she is unmarried? Of course not. Submission is necessary for any business, government, organization, or family to run smoothly. It prevents chaos. The term "too many Chiefs and not enough Indians" comes from having too many people unwilling to do the work while they all want to rule, resulting in nothing getting accomplished. That is what happens when no one is willing to be submissive.

What is meant by the word submissive? It is NOT surrender, withdrawal, or apathy. It is NOT inferiority. God created all people in His image, so all have equal value. Submission is mutual commitment and cooperation to achieve a common goal. God did not make man superior to woman. He made a way for them to work together without conflict. Jesus Christ is equal to God the Father, but submitted to Him to carry out the plan for salvation. Submission between equals is submission by choice, not by force.

Read 1 Corinthians 11:4-7

Paul is returning to his theme of how to conduct yourself as a Christian so as not to offend others and cause others to turn away from the church. It is not a Scriptural command for women to wear head coverings during worship. However, this was a cultural problem in Paul's day. It was customary in Greek and Eastern cities for women to cover their heads in public. Those who didn't were considered women of immoral character. Some of the Christian women felt they no longer needed to live under the Jewish law because they were set free from the law when they became Christians. They ceased wearing their head coverings and veils. This upset others within the church and was threatening to cause conflict within the church. So to keep peace, Paul tells the women to continue to cover their heads as was the custom.

When Paul talks about length of hair for men and women and hair coverings, he is saying Christians should behave in ways acceptable within their culture. Paul said, "...IF it is a disgrace for a woman to have her hair cut off or her head shaved, then she should cover her head."

Long or short hair is obviously relative according to the culture. In some societies long hair on men is considered appropriate and masculine. However, in Corinth it was considered a sign of male prostitution. Women with short hair were labeled prostitutes. Paul was saying in the Corinthian culture, Christian women should keep their hair long. A woman with short hair would find it more difficult to earn respect and be taken seriously as a believable witness for Christ. We should avoid appearances and behaviors which will detract from our ultimate goal of being believable witnesses for Jesus Christ.

Read 1 Corinthians 11:8-10

Angels are observers of our worship. They understand the heavenly hierarchy and would therefore understand the concept of a woman covering her head as a sign of submission. It would not be appropriate for a man to cover his head since "he is the image and glory of God," as Paul said in verse 7.

Read 1 Corinthians 11:11-12

Paul is reminding them of the equality of all people. Without men, there would be no women. Conversely, without women, there would be no men. We are all God's creation, and therefore equal in His sight.

Read 1 Corinthians 11:13-16

Paul repeats his stance to stress its importance. They did not have bold type or any other means of showing emphasis in their writings. So when something was important, they repeated it two, three, or more times. The more a point was repeated, the more important it was.

Paul says to judge for yourself if it is important for a woman to cover her head when she prays to God. Then he goes on to say, in the churches he had established, it was the practice for her to do so (because it was the custom of the day.)

Read 1 Corinthians 11:17-19

Paul has heard about disagreements within the church. He recognizes there will be differences of opinion within groups, but his concern is these differences may cause conflict and diminish their purpose of worshipping the Lord. Those who cause discord serve to highlight those who are genuine believers. As the saying goes, 'The cream always rises to the top.'

Read 1 Corinthians 11:20-22

The church in Corinth had lost sight of the purpose of the Lord's Supper. In addition to Communion, they would include huge feasts of fellowship. This fellowship meal had become a time of gluttony and excessive drinking for the rich among them, while the less fortunate went hungry. This certainly did not demonstrate the unity and love which should have been characteristic of the church, nor was it the proper preparation for Communion. Paul rebukes their practice and then goes on to remind them of the purpose of the Lord's Supper.

Read 1 Corinthians 11:23-26

Jesus instituted the Lord's Supper on the night of the Passover meal. Just as Passover celebrated deliverance from slavery in Egypt, so the Lord's Supper celebrates deliverance from sin by Christ's death. The bread represents Christ's body, and the wine represents His blood. Participating in the Lord's Supper is an important element in the Christian faith and strengthens us spiritually as we remember the basis of our beliefs.

In the old covenant, people could approach God only through the priests and the act of sacrifice. The death of Jesus on the cross created a new covenant, or agreement, between God and His people. "…the new covenant in my blood…" allow all people to personally approach God and communicate with Him. Eating the bread and drinking the cup shows we are remembering Christ's death for us and renewing our commitment to serve Him.

Read 1 Corinthians 11:27-29

Paul gives specific instructions on how we should approach the Lord's Supper.

1. We should make sure everyone is gathered together, and partake in an orderly and unified manner.
2. We should examine ourselves—consider if we are worthy. Are we heavy hearted about something? Then pray and lay it at the feet of the Lord. Is there sin in our life? Then repent of it. Any unconfessed sin or resentful attitudes—whatever is not right in our life—should be corrected before partaking in the bread and cup.
3. Next, we should remember Christ and His sacrifice for us, and take the Lord's Supper with due reverence and respect.

Paul was speaking to church members who were rushing into the Lord's Supper as a ritual without thinking about its meaning. Those who did so were not honoring Christ's sacrifice and shared in the guilt of those who crucified Jesus. We should prepare ourselves for Communion through introspection, confession of sin, and resolution of differences with others. This will remove the barriers affecting our relationship with Christ and with fellow believers.

Read 1 Corinthians 11:30-34

"Fallen asleep" is Paul's way of describing death. Paul describes disciplinary judgments to highlight the seriousness of the Communion sacrament. The Lord's Supper is not to be taken lightly. This new covenant cost Jesus his life. It is not a meaningless ritual, but a sacrament given by Christ to help strengthen our faith.

The Lord's Supper is a time of fellowship for believers and a time of remembrance. It is not a time to quench your thirst or alleviate your hunger. Paul says to eat beforehand so you can come to the fellowship meal in the right frame of mind.

He ends this portion of his letter by telling them he will give them further instruction on this subject when he sees them.

1 Corinthians – Chapter 12

Paul moves on to another topic as he continues his letter—the gifts of the Spirit.

Many of the gifts Paul talks about in this chapter may seem foreign to us today. Before the New Testament was completed, there was still a need for the Holy Spirit to give miraculous manifestations in the form of special gifts. This was necessary because the Apostles were few, the churches were far apart, ideas could travel no faster than people could at that time, and the churches were being overrun with false teachers. Without written records as to the actual facts, they had no way of knowing the truth except through the work of the Holy Spirit's gifts. Today, we have God's Holy Word, written by chosen ones with the help of the Holy Spirit, rendering some of those gifts unnecessary. Do they still exist? I don't have the answer to that. Only the Holy Spirit knows which gifts He bestows on each born again believer. It is our job to figure out which gift He has given each of us and use it to the best of our ability. But today we do have the New Testament Scriptures, which tell us how to discern false teachings from the truth. If they don't agree with the Scriptures, they are false.

Read 1 Corinthians 12:1

Paul begins this part of his letter with "now about…," which suggests he is answering another question the Corinthians raised in their letter to him.

Spiritual Gifts: a gift of grace from the Holy Spirit enabling one to minister to the needs of the body of Christ, the church.

Read 1 Corinthians 12:2

In the past, the Corinthians had been influenced to worship 'mute' idols. These idols did not speak or give guidance in any way. They were mere statuettes or figurines. But now they are led by the Holy Spirit.

Read 1 Corinthians 12:3

Paul used the Greek translation of the Old Testament Hebrew name "Yahweh." When the text was translated into English, it was translated as "Lord." Anyone possessing the Holy Spirit cannot put a curse on Jesus. But only someone possessing the Holy Spirit can confess Jesus as Lord from his/her heart.

Read 1 Corinthians 12:4-6

These verses reflect the Trinity. The Holy Spirit distributes gifts to those saved by grace.

The Lord Jesus is who we serve when we serve the church. The word used here for "serve" indicates service to the Christian community. The same word is later used for the office of deacon in Philippians 1:1.

The Greek word translated as "working" means "power that is in operation." God works within each of us in different ways. He helps us use our spiritual gifts to produce obvious results.

Read 1 Corinthians 12:7

Every member of the body of Christ is given a spiritual gift as evidence of the Holy Spirit working in his/her life. All of the gifts together are intended to build up the Christian community. They are not to be used selfishly. Paul probably mentions this because some of the Corinthians were using their gifts for profit or fame, or bragging that their gift is more superior than someone else's, and therefore they must be more spiritual. We must never use gifts as a means to manipulate others or serve our own self-interest.

Read 1 Corinthians 12:8-11

The Greek word translated as 'tongues' also means 'languages.' On the day of Pentecost, the apostles were able to understand and speak the different languages and dialects of different groups of people.

All Christians have faith, but verse 9 is speaking of faith to meet a specific need within the body of Christ. The Greek word translated as "gifts of healing" should have been translated in the plural, "gifts of healings." The double plural indicates several kinds of illnesses and various ways God heals them.

In verse 10, we read about how some have 'miraculous powers,' or deeds of power. In Scripture, a miracle is an action unexplained by natural means. It is an act of God as evidence of His power and purpose.

Another gift is that of prophesy, which is the communication from the mind of God imparted to a believer by the Holy Spirit in the form of a prediction or an indication of the will of God in a particular situation.

"Distinguishing between spirits" is the ability to tell the difference between truth from the Holy Spirit and falsehoods from evil spirits. This ability usually reveals itself through fervent prayer and study of Scripture.

Read 1 Corinthians 12:12

Not everyone has the same gift. The Holy Spirit distributes the gifts as He determines they are needed. It may be a gift of knowledge of the scripture, or a gift of organization, or a gift of interpreting other languages, or the gift of caring for others, or one of many other gifts. Each of us is different and has been given different abilities and strengths. If your gift is working to collect food and goods for the needy, that's what you need to concentrate on doing. However, if someone else does not share your passion for that particular job and will not help with that chore, don't accuse that person of not serving. His/her gift may be leading them in a different direction to serve in another capacity. That's what makes the body function properly. Each part working to do their part in the way it was intended.

Read 1 Corinthians 12:13

It doesn't matter what our background might be, once we become a part of the body of Christ through the baptism of the Holy Spirit, we are all given the same love and grace from our Lord. We are equal in His sight. There is no discrimination.

Read 1 Corinthians 12:14-20

All gifts are important. Some in the Corinthian church felt some gifts were more important than others, but Paul tells them none of the gifts are inferior to others. An ear is as important as an eye. A foot is as important as a hand. The same is true of the gifts of the Holy Spirit. When all the parts work together, the entire body of Christ—the church—runs smoothly with Christ as the head leading us. This diversity of gifts is intended to accomplish God's unified purpose.

God uses diversity to create unity. What a wonderful concept!

Read 1 Corinthians 12:21-25

This was written to those who feel their gifts were insignificant. Paul explains that some parts of the body may seem weak, but they are actually indispensable. Just as we feed our stomachs (which no one sees and therefore it may seem unimportant) we should give honor and support to the Christians in the church who have seemingly ordinary gifts. Christians whose functions may be obscure in the church are to be given special respect. Those with more obvious gifts do not need to be given special honor.

Read 1 Corinthians 12:26

There should be mutual respect between each member of the body of Christ so there will be no divisions within the church. When there is discord, the entire body of the church suffers. When we show honor and respect for one another, everyone rejoices.

Read 1 Corinthians 12:27-31

All have different gifts. Everyone cannot expect to be given the same gift. Some will be teachers, some prophets, some helpers, and others healers. Paul's list seems to be random, possibly naming those gifts most desired or looked upon by the Corinthians to be most important. Apparently, the Corinthians were seeking status according to the gifts they were given, but Paul explains they should follow his advice from this letter. He does not list love as a gift. It is rather a fruit of the Spirit. By showing love for each other and not competing with one another according to their gifts, they will find it to be "the most excellent way," which Paul continues to explain in the next chapter.

Using the same analogy Paul used, we can take it a step further. An eye is an important part of the body. Yes, the body can function without it, but eyes enhance the body's experience. However, is the eye any good without the body? Of course not. You may have a gift and feel you can use it without being a part of a church. But without the body, the single part loses its importance and function. It cannot be productive without the body. It cannot survive if isolated from the rest. All parts must cooperate to form a single, unified body.

1 Corinthians – Chapter 13

This is probably the most well-known chapter in the Bible because it is so often used in weddings. However, when Paul wrote it, he was not talking about the love between man and woman. He was referring to love on a much broader sense—heavenly love—the kind of love Jesus showed us when He walked the earth. People were drawn to Him because of His immense love for mankind. His love was a manifestation of God's Power. Love is the church's most effective weapon. Without love, all of the various gifts of the Spirit are worthless. Love is the essence of God's nature. Love is the perfection of human character and ultimately the most powerful force in the universe.

The Corinthians were using the gifts given them by the Holy Spirit to show their importance rather than using them in love. They were boastful and fought among themselves about which gifts were the most important. Paul explains to them why love is more important than all the gifts. Although people have different gifts, love is available to everyone.

Read 1 Corinthians 13:1-3

If we give everything we have to feed the poor, but do not have love, it means nothing. Even if we possess all the gifts such as speaking in other languages of men or in the language of the angels, or the gift of prophesying, or the gift of possessing all knowledge, or have the faith to move mountains, or even if we give up all earthly possessions, or even martyrdom, it is all worthless unless we have the spirit of Christian love. Love should be our motivation in all things.

The Greek word for this kind of love means 'a selfless concern for the welfare of others, irrespective of the lovableness in the person loved, but the product of a will to love in obedience to God's command.' It is like Christ's love manifested on the cross.

Read 1 Corinthians 13:4-7

Humans tend to confuse love with lust. We *love* chocolate, or we *love* sports. We see love as a way of fulfilling ourselves. But God's kind of love is directed outward toward others, not inward toward ourselves. It is unselfish, going against our natural tendencies. We can only practice this type of love by setting aside our own desires. True Godly love is given without expecting something in return. The more we become like Christ, the more love we will show toward others.

Read 1 Corinthians 13:8-12

We are given spiritual gifts for our lives on earth to build up, serve, and strengthen fellow Christians. When we leave this world and enter into the presence of God, we will be made perfect and complete with no need for those spiritual gifts. They are to be used on earth for the advancement of the Church, to make it stronger and help spread the message of Christ.

Paul gives us a glimpse into heaven. He says we don't have all the answers now, but when we see God face-to-face, we will fully understand everything for we will see things from God's perspective. This truth should strengthen our faith and resolve.

Read 1 Corinthians 13:13

Faith is the foundation and content of God's message to mankind. Hope is the attitude and focus we obtain through our faith. Love is the action we express when our faith and hope are in line.

Not only is love the greatest because of its importance in making everything else worthwhile, but long after all of the spiritual gifts are no longer necessary, love will remain the governing principle in everything God and His redeemed people are and do.

In morally corrupt Corinth, love had become an overused term without meaning. Today, we still overuse and misuse the word, diminishing its significance. Love is the greatest of all human qualities. It is the essence of God. If our faith and hope are aligned, we understand how God loves and are free to love completely.

1 Corinthians – Chapter 14

Read 1 Corinthians 14:1-5

Spiritual gifts can only be effective through love. Gifts were given in order to spread the gospel and build up the church.

The gift of prophecy may involve predicting of future events, but its main purpose is to communicate God's message to people, providing insight, warning, correction, and encouragement.

Speaking in tongues was causing disorder in worship because the Corinthian believers were using it improperly. If someone has been given the gift to speak in other languages, then remains in his church and goes around speaking in a language no one understands without using an interpreter, what good is he doing? He was given the gift to speak in other languages so he could go preach to those who would understand that language. Therefore, someone who has the gift of prophecy is greater than the one speaking in a foreign language without an interpreter. What is spoken in the church must be intelligible to the listeners. Paul is not saying the gift of tongues is unimportant, only that it must be used properly to improve the morals or knowledge of the church members. If used properly, this gift is as important as the gift of prophecy. All gifts should be used to unify and strengthen the church, not to make ourselves feel good.

Read 1 Corinthians 14:6-9

One note repeated over and over does not accomplish anything. It does not create a recognizable tune. In order to recognize and appreciate a particular tune, the notes must be arranged in a way as to create a meaningful tune. Flutes and harps were well known instruments in Greece. The trumpet was used for battle signals. The notes sounded would convey a message. The same is true with the use of a foreign language. If the people cannot understand what you are saying, it is of no value unless there is an interpreter.

Read 1 Corinthians 14:10-14

All languages in the world have meaning to those who understand them. But when you speak in front of a group of people who do not comprehend the language you're using, you are not accomplishing anything. Paul also says if those with the gift of tongues pray without understanding their own words, their spirit prays, but their mind remains unchanged. This verse suggests it was possible those who spoke in tongues didn't even understand what they were saying. Then language was foreign to them, even though they spoke it.

Read 1 Corinthians 14:15-17

Praying, singing, praising God, thanksgiving, and saying "Amen" are all elements of worship employed in the Old Testament. The Greek word for inquirer is a technical term for someone not fully initiated into a religion. Saying "Amen" (meaning "it is true" or "so be it") is the believer's confession of agreement with the words spoken.

If the believer or listener does not understand what is being said, how can they agree? We must pray and sing (worship) with both mind and spirit in order to lift up others within the church.

Read 1 Corinthians 14:18-19

Paul obviously possessed the gift of speaking in other languages. He traveled all over the region spreading the gospel, so it was necessary for him to be able to speak different languages in his travels so each culture would be able to understand his message. But whenever he was in a church, he would speak in the language that congregation would understand rather than show off his knowledge of many languages.

Read 1 Corinthians 14:20-22

Verse 21 is a quote from Isaiah 28:11-12. Whenever Paul quotes from the Old Testament, he refers to it as "The Law." This passage from Isaiah indicated the foreign language of the Assyrians was a sign to unbelieving Israel that judgment was coming on them. Paul concluded from this that speaking in tongues was intended to be a sign for unbelievers. Prophecy was for believers since it revealed truth to those who received it.

Paul says, "In regard to evil be infants." Babies have no wrong motives. They have needs of comfort, but no ulterior motives. As infants, we should not have any evil desires in wanting to excel in spiritual gifts to inflate our own egos or puff ourselves up. Gifts were not given to increase our stance in society, but were given to be used in elevating the church and spreading the gospel of Christ.

Then he says, "But in your thinking be adults." As adults we can reason and use our minds to comprehend the message God gives us through His Word and prophecy.

Read 1 Corinthians 14:23-25

Inquirers are referred to in some manuscripts as "some who do not understand." Inquirers were those who wanted to know more about the gospel, but had not yet come to understand it all. Unbelievers were those who understood, but had not yet accepted. If these two groups entered a church meeting where everyone was speaking in foreign languages, they would be repulsed by the confusion, causing a negative effect rather than the intended impressive sign.

Prophesying, although intended for believers, is spoken in the native language and would therefore have a positive effect on unbelievers because they hear and understand and are convicted of their sins.

Read 1 Corinthians 14:26-28

When they came together to worship, it is apparent they all took part, not just certain leaders or officers. Hymns, words of instruction, revelations or prophecies, and speaking in foreign languages with interpretations were all elements of worship in the Corinthian church. All of these must be used to strengthen the church.

Paul imparted three restrictions, or rules, for those speaking in other languages in the church service: Only two or three should do so in a meeting, they should do so one at a time, and there must be an interpreter.

Read 1 Corinthians 14:29-33

As with those speaking in tongues, the prophets also were given rules: Only two or three should speak in the service, one at a time. While one is speaking the others were to consider what they said carefully and decide the validity of his message. If another prophet stood to speak, the first must sit down and allow the second to take the floor. This avoided confusion for those listening.

Speaking in tongues and prophesying was not an uncontrollable emotional moment of ecstasy. Paul says these gifts should be controlled by those possessing them. Forethought needed to be applied before using their gifts. Paul reminds them how God is a God of peace, not of disorder. Worship services should always be orderly, not disruptive or confusing. When there is chaos, the church is not allowing God to work among believers as He would like. God had called believers in Christ to peace and unity. Paul was concerned about how disorderly and unregulated worship at Corinth would discredit God's people.

Now we come to a controversial verse in our present day society.

Read 1 Corinthians 14:34-35

"All congregations of the saints" stresses the collective unity of the entire visible church of God on earth. All congregations are to obey the directive given here.

The culture of that time in Corinth dictated it was disrespectful for women to confront men in public. Paul's concern was for believers to be respectful of one another and of God as they exercised their spiritual gifts. Even in their culture, there were times when a woman was allowed to participate in worship. In 1 Corinthians 11:5, Paul indicates women did possess the gift of prophecy, and therefore would be allowed to pray and prophesy in church. Paul's purpose was not to define a woman's role within the worship service, but to establish a fitting and orderly way of worship.

Paul is not altogether forbidding women to speak in church, but is forbidding the disorderly discussions and clamoring for explanations. They were allowed to participate in worship, but not to have public confrontations. Apparently, some of the women who had become Christians believed their Christian freedom from the law gave them the right to question the men in public worship. This was causing division in the church. Paul suggests they should wait until they get home to discuss things with their husbands rather than disrupt the worship services.

Read 1 Corinthians 14:36-38

Paul is being sarcastic in asking rhetorical questions. He accuses the Corinthians of following their own practices rather than conforming to God's Word. He also points out that any of them who genuinely possess gifts from God will recognize Paul's God-given authority and recognize his commands are the Lord's commands. Anyone who does not accept these commands and disobeys them will be treated as an unbeliever.

Read 1 Corinthians 14:39-40

Paul ends this portion of his letter by stressing it is not his purpose to forbid speaking in tongues, but to make sure the gift is used correctly, with interpreters. He repeats his purpose for writing, which is to restore order within the worship services.

1 Corinthians – Chapter 15

This chapter is the fullest discussion of the resurrection of Jesus in the New Testament. It is one of the most significant chapters in the Bible giving meaning to human life. Without the resurrection, the mystery of our existence would be an unsolved riddle, leaving nothing but the emptiness and blackness of eternal despair. But the resurrection of Jesus from the dead is the one most important and best established fact in all history. The story has come down to us through the centuries, and as we study this chapter, you will see why it is such an established fact.

Read 1 Corinthians 15:1-2

Paul is saying not to let go of your belief in the gospel, hold firmly to it, and faithfully follow Jesus, to retain your salvation.

Read 1 Corinthians 15:3-6

The crucifixion of the Messiah was foretold by early scriptures, and Christ's death happened exactly as it was prophesied. The resurrection of Jesus was witnessed by many including Peter and the disciples. Then Jesus appeared to a crowd of 500 people at one time. At the writing of this letter, many of those 500 were still living since it had only been about 27 years since it had happened. A crowd of 500 people could not have all imagined the same thing at the same time, so it must have been a real occurrence.

Verse 4 says, "...he was raised on the third day...." The Jews counted parts of days as whole days, so the three days would include part of Friday afternoon, all of Saturday, and Sunday morning.

There have been many theories through the years to explain away Christ's resurrection, but all of them fall short of disproving it in light of the evidence. There will always be people who say Jesus didn't rise from the dead, but the resurrection is an historical fact, witnessed by over 520 people. The Gospel books (Matthew, Mark, Luke, and John) list more witnesses than are listed here.

Read 1 Corinthians 15:7-9

The resurrected body of Jesus was also seen by His brother, James, and all of the apostles. James did not believe Jesus was the Messiah until he saw his brother raised from the dead. Then he became a believer, ultimately a leader of the church in Jerusalem, and provided us with the book of James.

Last of all, Jesus appeared to Paul on the road to Damascus, which was several years after Christ's death. When Paul says he was as one abnormally born, he means he was a special case. He was not a follower of Jesus as were the other apostles. Paul's life changed because of his encounter with Jesus. Before that day, Paul, then known as Saul, was a persecutor of Christians. But once he saw Jesus raised from the dead, he could deny him no longer and became an apostle and the author of the majority of our New Testament books.

Read 1 Corinthians 15:10

Although Paul knew he had worked hard and accomplished a lot, he was humble. He knew it was only due to God's grace and kindness that he was able to achieve all he had done. Paul was not being boastful when he said he had worked harder than all the rest, but was acknowledging he had to make up for his past transgressions as a persecutor of Christians. He had a much more difficult time convincing people of his belief in the gospel since they knew of his past.

Read 1 Corinthians 15:11-12

These verses indicate there were false teachers within the church in Corinth who were saying Christ was not raised from the dead. Most Greeks did not believe bodies would be resurrected after death. They believed it was something that happened only to the soul. They believed the soul was imprisoned in a physical body and was only released through death. Since the church in Corinth was in the heart of Greek culture, many believers had a difficult time letting go of this belief to grasp the idea that our body and soul will be reunited after our resurrection.

Read 1 Corinthians 15:13-18

Paul points out to the Corinthian church, if Christ did not conquer death, there is no basis for the existence of Christianity or the Church. The resurrection is the center of the Christian faith. Christ rose from the dead as He promised, so we know He is God as He said. Because He rose, we have certainty our sins are forgiven and He lives and represents us to God. We also know, because He rose and defeated death, we also will be raised.

Read 1 Corinthians 15:19

In Paul's day, there were few benefits for being a Christian in that society. It brought persecution, ostracism from family, and in many cases, poverty. It certainly was not a step up the social ladder. But even more important, if Christ did not conquer death, Christians could not be forgiven for sins and would have no hope of eternal life.

Read 1 Corinthians 15:20

"Firstfruits" were the first, and best, part of the harvest. Jesus was indeed the first to be raised from the grave and enter heaven.

Read 1 Corinthians 15:21-22

Death entered the world because of Adam's sin.

Read Romans 5:12

Thus Christ had to become a man in order to overcome death and bring salvation to mankind.

Read Romans 5:17-21

Read 1 Corinthians 15:23-27

Now when it says that "everything" has been put under him, it is clear this does not include God himself, who put everything under Christ.

Read 1 Corinthians 15:28

Here Paul gives us a glimpse into the future, when Christ's job as our mediator is finished and the universe enters its final stage. Jesus was given a job to do by His Father, which is to defeat all evil on earth. First He defeated sin and death on the cross, and in the final days,

He will defeat Satan and all evil.

Verse 27 comes from Psalm 8:6. "Everything under His feet" is an Old Testament term meaning complete conquest.

Read 1 Corinthians 15:29

Being baptized for an unbaptized loved one who has passed is something some other faiths still practice today. However, this is the only time it is mentioned in the scriptures. Paul's point is that this practice certainly affirms a belief in resurrection.

Read 1 Corinthians 15:30-32

Here Paul quotes Isaiah 22:13 to make his point. If there is no resurrection, why were they endangering themselves by preaching the gospel? If death ended it all, they may as well enjoy the moment, for that would be all that matters.

Read 1 Corinthians 15:33

Paul quotes the poet, Menander, from the Greek comedy, "Thais." Paul is warning them to not keep company with those who were preaching against the resurrection. We cannot allow our relationships with nonbelievers lead us away from Christ or cause our faith to waver.

Read 1 Corinthians 15:34

Paul accuses them of sinning by doubting the resurrection of Christ. He says this is a shameful situation for them to listen to others who are ignorant of God.

Read 1 Corinthians 15:35-38

This is among my favorite passages of the Bible because it explains the process of our change from mortal to immortal. Paul explains, when we sow seeds, they grow into plants, which are an improvement upon the original seed. When we "plant" our earthly bodies, God will produce a new unblemished body of like kind—an improvement over the original.

Read 1 Corinthians 15:39

Some believe animals don't go to heaven. I'm not so sure because this verse seems to say God will raise each "planted" body according to the type of flesh it was on earth. As we read on, notice verse 44.

Read 1 Corinthians 15:40-44

"IF there is a natural body, there is also a spiritual body." Animals have natural bodies, so why wouldn't this verse hold true for them?

Our resurrected bodies will be different in some ways, but not all, from our earthly bodies. We will be recognizable in our new spiritual body, yet it will be better than we can imagine. It will be made to live forever. We will have our own personalities and individualities, but we will be without sickness or disease. Our present bodies are perishable and prone to decay. Our new bodies will not be weak, will never get sick, will never die, and will not be limited by the laws of nature, making them more capable than our earthly bodies. We cannot know exactly what this means, but it definitely sounds like something to look forward to.

Read 1 Corinthians 15:45-49

In verse 45, Paul quotes Genesis 2:7.
"The first man" was Adam, the first earthly man.

We were all made in the same fashion, from the dust of the earth, the same as Adam.

"The heavenly man," or "the last Adam," was Jesus, the life-giving spirit. Just as Jesus was given a heavenly body, so will we.

Our hope is not merely immortality of the spirit, but actual resurrection of the body. New Testament teaching is very plain on this. We will not have the same corrupt earthly bodies we have now, but more complete and perfected spiritual bodies.

Read 1 Corinthians 15:50

This verse makes it clear we will not enter heaven until we have received our perfected body. However, the following verses explain how that happens in a "twinkling of an eye."

Read 1 Corinthians 15:51-54

In this last line, Paul quotes from Isaiah 25:8.

"We will not all sleep" means the Christians who are alive when Christ returns to gather His people will be transformed into their imperishable bodies without experiencing death.

Read 1 Corinthians 15:55

This is a quote from Hosea 13:14.

Read 1 Corinthians 15:56-57

Satan seemed to be victorious in the Garden of Eden and at the cross of Jesus. But God turned Satan's victory into defeat when Jesus rose from the dead. Death is no longer a source of dread or fear. Death has been defeated, giving us hope beyond the grave.

F.A.C.T.S.

Read 1 Corinthians 15:58

Because of the resurrection, our work for the Lord is not in vain. Sometimes we hesitate to do things we know we should because we don't see any results. We need to keep a heavenly perspective, realizing we often will not see the good that comes from our efforts. We must allow God to use us by continuing to do those things we know are right. His wisdom reaches beyond our limited awareness. Do the good you have opportunity to do knowing your work will have eternal results.

1 Corinthians – Chapter 16

In the last chapter, Paul reminded the members of the Corinthian church their labor was not in vain. In this chapter, he gives examples of practical deeds all Christians should practice.

Read 1 Corinthians 16:1-4

Because he begins with "now about," we know he was again responding to one of their questions. Christians in Jerusalem were suffering from poverty and famine, and Paul was greatly concerned about them. He brings it up several times in his letters. He mentions taking up a collection for them here, in Romans and in 2 Corinthians. Paul's objective was to deliver the money the churches collected to the Jerusalem church.

The letter to the Galatians does not mention Paul's instruction of collecting for the poor. Paul must have told them to do so in person, or there may have been another letter which was not preserved.

"On the first day of every week" was the established day for Christians to worship as described in Acts 20:7. There are written accounts from 150 A.D. of people bringing their offerings to church on Sundays.

The churches chose and approved certain men to be responsible for the funds collected. Paul suggests he might accompany those men to Jerusalem to deliver the gift.

Read 1 Corinthians 16:5-9

The word "Pentecost" means "50," (the 50th day) referring to the 50 days after Passover, when the Jews celebrated the Feast of Firstfruits in the late spring of the year. So Paul is writing this letter in the spring before Pentecost somewhere around 55 - 57 A.D. He spent the summer in Macedonia and went to Corinth in the fall, where he stayed through the winter. Paul had indicated previously in his letter he did not want to be a financial burden to them, so when he mentions them helping him on his journey, he is probably referring to supplies and equipment, as well as prayers.

Read 1 Corinthians 16:10-11

Timothy, although young and somewhat timid, had worked closely with Paul and earned his respect and trust. Paul planned to send Timothy ahead to Corinth and asked the Corinthian church to welcome him because he was doing God's work. God's work is not limited by age.

1 Timothy and 2 Timothy are letters Paul wrote to Timothy.

Paul refers to "brothers" who were traveling with Timothy. We know there was a believer from Corinth named Erastus who traveled with Timothy at times. Erastus was the city's director of public works. In Acts we learn he was one of the brothers Paul referred to here.

Read 1 Corinthians 16:12

The members of the church in Corinth had inquired about whether Apollos would be visiting them. Paul tells them he asked Apollos to go to Corinth, but Apollos was hesitant to go there because he knew of the problems they were having with false teachers and arguments within the church. Not wanting to get involved in the situation and not wanting to cause more division within the Corinthian church, Apollos had declined.

Read 1 Corinthians 16:13-14

To those within the church, Paul instructed them about what they should do while they awaited his return. As we wait for the return of Christ, we should be following these same instructions:
1. Be on guard against spiritual dangers;
2. Stand firm in the faith;
3. Behave courageously;
4. Be strong;
5. Do everything with kindness and in love.

Read 1 Corinthians 16:15-18

The household of Stephanas was among the first Paul had baptized. For Paul to bring them up and defend their faithfulness indicates the Corinthians were not very fond of them. There may have been some biases, discriminations, or other reasons they were not accepted, but Paul urges them to realize that anyone who is devoted to serving the Lord and His people are worthy of respect. These may have been the ones to deliver the letter from the Corinthian church to Paul because he says he was glad when they arrived. They supplied what he was lacking from the Corinthian church by showing him the affection he desired from their entire church. By being willing to come to Paul and get advice from him to take back to the church members, they had restored his spirit.

Read 1 Corinthians 16:19

The province of Asia was the Roman province (now in western Turkey) in which Ephesus and the surrounding cities were located. During Paul's ministry in Ephesus, all of that area heard the Word, including the churches of Colossae, Laodicea, and Hierapolis, which were located on the border of the province of Asia.

Aquila and Priscilla were tentmakers whom Paul had met in Corinth. They followed him to Ephesus and lived there with him helping to teach others about Jesus. Many in the Corinthian church would have been familiar with this couple since they had helped Paul establish the church in Corinth. Paul also mentions them in Acts 18:18, Romans 16:3, and 2 Timothy 4:19. They held church in their home in Ephesus. Holding church services in their homes was not unusual during this period of time. When we talk about Paul "establishing churches," we are referring to a group of people meeting together in homes. There were no church buildings erected.

Read 1 Corinthians 16:20

In Paul's day, kissing was a normal way to greet each other. Paul encouraged the "holy kiss," a kiss of mutual respect and love in the Lord, as a way for Christians to greet each other and reduce the tension caused by divisions within the church.

Read 1 Corinthians 16:21

Paul had an assistant, or "scribe", to whom he dictated his letters. However, these final words were written in his own handwriting. It was his way of personalizing the letter and served to verify this was a genuine letter from him and not a forgery.

Read 1 Corinthians 16:22

For those who did not love the Lord, Paul's wish for them was to endure God's displeasure and wrath because of their lack of love and obedience to God. The word translated here as "curse" does not mean the type of curse a witch would perform. Jesus forbid that type of curse.

The Greek for "Come, Lord" (Marana tha) was an Aramaic expression used by early Christians.

Paul was excited about Christ coming back to earth again. He was not afraid of seeing Christ – in fact, he could hardly wait. Those who love Christ are looking forward to His return.

Do you share Paul's eager anticipation of seeing Christ one day?

Read 1 Corinthians 16:23-24

In his letter to Corinth, Paul lovingly, but forcefully, confronted the problems the church had and pointed them back to Christ. Divisions and conflicts, selfishness, wrongful use of their freedom, disorder in their worship, misuse of their spiritual gifts, and wrong attitudes toward the resurrection were some of the situations he wrote to them about. Every church has problems, causing tensions and divisions. We need to deal with them head on as Paul did.

The book of 1 Corinthians teaches us that unity and love within a church are far more important than leaders and labels.

2 Corinthians

Paul probably wrote this second Corinthian letter about 6 months after 1 Corinthians. It contains his message of thanksgiving and love. He describes the tribulations he has suffered while preaching the gospel of Christ. As we study this book, compare the difficulties he faced with the minimal hardships we endure for Christ.

Acts 19 tells us more about Paul during this period of time.

Read Acts 19:8-20

Paul worked for two years and 3 months at Ephesus. This was the longest period of time Paul stayed in one place during his missionary journeys. He spoke in the synagogue for the first 3 months, but his teaching of "The Way" was publicly mocked and ridiculed. So for the remaining two years he held daily discussions in the lecture hall and performed healings and driving out evil spirits. Lecture halls were used for schooling children or used by philosophers, which was usually done in the cooler early time of day, so Paul probably had to hold his lectures during the heated afternoons.

His strategy throughout his missionary journeys was to go to the larger hub cities as central locations where he could draw the largest audience. Those who came to hear him would return to the surrounding areas and spread the Gospel.

Ephesus is where he begins his third journey. By the middle of 2 Corinthians, he has traveled to Macedonia, so he may have written this letter during or after his third missionary journey.

The purpose of these letters was to follow up on the spiritual growth of the converts he'd left in Corinth.

What kind of 'follow up' work do we do for the new Christians in our church and community? Do we rejoice when they are baptized and then leave them on their own? Most of us do. And that is why there are so many who drift back into their old lifestyle rather than grow in spiritual strength.

It should be common sense for us to help the 'newborn' Christian grow. The practice of the apostle Paul to keep in contact with his fellow Christians reveals to us it should be both a spiritual and Scriptural responsibility for us to continue to help those who are won to Christ until they reach maturity.

2 Corinthians – Chapter 1

In Acts, we learn how Paul made it a practice to re-visit the churches he had founded. As we begin this book, the church of Corinth is about to enter its seventh year of existence. It's 57 AD and Paul has spent a couple of years in Ephesus, keeping in close contact with the church by sending Timothy, and later Titus, to visit them and bring back word from them. Now he feels the need to visit them himself, but writes this letter before doing so. Its main purpose was to give the church the opportunity to straighten things out for themselves before he arrived to straighten them out his way.

Read 2 Corinthians 1:1

Evidently, Timothy was with Paul at the time he wrote this letter.

Achaia refers to Greece, as opposed to the northern Macedonia. Although he is writing to those in Corinth, he also intends for this letter to be read by the other churches in that area.

Read 2 Corinthians 1:2-4

Some people blame God for allowing tribulations in our lives. Others praise Him for keeping us from tribulations. Most of us see tribulations as something to be avoided at all costs, but Paul saw them as an integral part of Christian life. He didn't see God's comfort as his own personal prize. He viewed it as a means to comfort others. If you have been comforted by God, you have an obligation to extend a word of comfort to your fellow Christians who are also going through trials.

Just as a hurt child needs a parent's comfort, we go to our Heavenly Father to have Him kiss away the pain so we can be comforted.

Read 2 Corinthians 1:5

The sufferings a Christian endures are felt by Christ—he is our head and we the body. He feels our pain. In Acts 9:4, Christ asks "why persecutest thou me?" Just as nothing can separate us from the love of Christ, so our tribulations can be comforted by Him. You cannot "out-suffer" God's comfort.

Read 2 Corinthians 1:6-9

Without sorrows and heartaches of this life, we would never know what a faithful Father we have. Without dangers we would never know His ability to deliver. So God permits us to come to the end of ourselves to help us understand we should not trust in ourselves, but in Him.

In verse 8, "brothers and sisters" is translated from the Greek word "adelphoi" referring to believers, both men and women, as part of God's family.

Read 2 Corinthians 1:10-11

Paul thanks the Corinthians for praying for him. Whether we understand it or not, we should pray for those who are troubled and in despair. God does hear and answer our prayers.

Read 2 Corinthians 1:12-14

Originally Paul had planned to cross over by sea from Ephesus to Corinth to visit the Corinthians before going on to Macedonia, and then return back to them on his return trip, giving them the benefit of two visits. But he had a change of plans, and those who opposed him tried to convince the church in Corinth that his word could not be trusted; that he was unreliable because he didn't follow through with what he had told them. In the following verses, he explains his plans to visit them had not been abandoned, only modified.

Read 2 Corinthians 1:15-19

Paul says since they have believed, they have learned God is faithful and they have experienced the gospels dynamic power. He also reminds them God has made promises and will always be faithful to those promises.

Read 2 Corinthians 1:20

When we say "Amen" at the end of our prayers, what are we actually saying? "Amen" means "so be it" because we are to have faith that if we ask for it, it shall be resolved according to God's will because God promised to answer our prayers. Whatever His answer, we are to have faith it is taken care of—maybe not in the way we expected or wanted, but in the BEST possible way, God's way, through His wisdom.

Read 2 Corinthians 1:21-22

The Holy Spirit is a deposit from God as a promise of more to come. A deposit is a first installment (of our inheritance) and assures the recipient the rest is forthcoming.

Read 2 Corinthians 1:23-24

Paul explains his reason for not returning for his second visit was to spare them the pain he was experiencing. He had gone through something causing him to fear for his life, and he didn't want them to endure the same hardship. We are never told to what he's referring. It is possible this was explained in another letter that may have been lost. His change of plans was not because of a fickle and insensitive attitude, but was done out of love and concern for them.

2 Corinthians – Chapter 2

Read 2 Corinthians 2:1

Paul's original plan was to travel to Corinth on his way to Macedonia and then again on his way back from there. So somewhere between the writing of 1 Corinthians and the writing of 2 Corinthians he has visited them on his way to Macedonia, but did not go back to visit on his way back as planned. Here he says the first visit was so painful he couldn't bear to re-visit.

Read 2 Corinthians 2:2-4

His reference to a letter he had written, which obviously upset some of the members of the church, could have been 1 Corinthians. Some theologians believe there may have been another letter written between 1 and 2 Corinthians that has been lost. He says here his intent was not to upset them, but to show his love for them.

Read 2 Corinthians 2:5-11

Some theologians believe Paul is speaking of a particular incident here. Someone within the church has committed a serious offense and the Church has disciplined him. Some believe Paul is still referring to the man mentioned in 1 Corinthians 5:1-3.

Paul tells them their punishment was enough and they shouldn't continue to berate this person. He has shown genuine sorrow for his actions and has repented and therefore, the punishment should be discontinued and he should be lovingly restored into their fellowship. Although Church discipline is important, it should not be allowed to develop into a form of graceless rigor in which there's no room for forgiveness and restoration. Discipline should always be exercised in love, not done in anger. There is no place for a holier-than-thou attitude. This will only cause bitterness and resentment rather than the desired repentance.

Satan is cunning. He uses church members to cause unrest and dissatisfaction within the church. In many churches today there are members who carry the Bible under one arm and the church constitution under the other. But they pay more attention to the man-made document than to the Bible. So business meetings are filled with hassles over points of order and the will of the majority is restricted by ridiculous rules of that particular church. Even a slight deviation from the printed bulletin causes some to go into a rant. Although we need order within the service, these rules and documents made by man are not always inspired. There are times when the Holy Spirit my lead the service into another direction.

This is what happened with Paul. Although his PLAN was to visit them twice, it caused a lot of turmoil within the church when those plans changed.

This criticism of Paul being fickle because he changed his travel plans seems trivial enough. Why not simply ignore it? Because there was more at stake than Paul's personal reputation. His message of grace was also being questioned.

Have you ever heard the term "poisoning the well"? "Poisoning the well" means to attack someone's character if you can't come up with an argument against his claims. This tactic is used in courts a lot, and we've certainly seen enough examples of it during political campaigns! If a witness has a strong testimony against a defendant, then the attorney will try to discredit him as a viable witness. This is what those who were against Paul were doing. They couldn't argue against his message, so they were trying to discredit his apostleship. Therefore, Paul found it necessary to defend himself and explain his reasons for his change of plans.

Paul's delayed visit had accomplished a purpose. A church needs to be able to handle problems internally, not depend on anyone outside of the church to 'fix' things. By Paul staying away, the church members disciplined the offending member and did it in such a way as to cause him to see his error and repent. Paul was proud of them for this. The purpose of discipline within a church is to bring the person to repentance, not to get even or rid the church of that person. A vengeful attitude is forbidden by Scripture—vengeance belongs to God.

Read Galatians 6:1

Matthew 18:15-20 tells us there are four steps in discipline:
1. go to the individual alone to reason with him;
2. take a witness the second time;
3. take the matter to the church;
4. excommunicate him.

If at any time along the way, the person repents, the process stops and he is welcomed back and shown tender loving care so he can be restored.

Read 2 Corinthians 2:12-13

After his brief visit to Corinth (on his way to Macedonia), he went to Troas, a city on the Aegean coast, hoping to find Titus there. But he didn't find Titus, so Paul continued on to Macedonia. Notice Paul refers to Titus as his brother. Titus and Paul were not related by blood, but Paul held him in high esteem and entrusted him with the collection of funds for the poverty-stricken Christians of Jerusalem. He also chose him to carry this letter to the Corinthians.

Although the people in Troas were welcoming and seemed eager to embrace Paul's teachings, he decided to leave. Acts 16:8-10 tells us why: "[8]So they passed by Mysia and went down to Troas. [9]During the night Paul had a vision of a man of Macedonia standing and begging him, 'Come over to Macedonia and help us.' [10]After Paul had seen the vision, we got ready at once to leave for Macedonia, concluding that God had called us to preach the gospel to them."

An open door doesn't always mean it is God's will for you. It is physically impossible for us to enter every door that opens for us. We must rely on God's guidance to know which opportunities we should pursue.

If you have a problem in one area and another opportunity presents itself, this doesn't always mean it is God's will for you to leave the problem and go elsewhere. Who would have blamed Paul if he gave up on Corinth, with all their problems, and stayed in Troas where everyone was welcoming and wanted to learn? But God wanted Paul to move on and take care of the problems within the already established church.

On the other hand, when Christians cause problems, they can hinder God's work. If the church in Corinth had been spiritual, Paul could have stayed and preached in Troas and brought more people to Christ.

At this point, Paul stops his narrative of his itinerary and digresses. But this lengthy digression (which goes through chapter 7) is still relevant to the main point of this letter.

F.A.C.T.S.

Read 2 Corinthians 2:14-15

Paul describes the church as being led by God. Paul is describing the scene of a Roman triumph in which the victorious general would lead his soldiers and the captives they had taken in a festive parade, while the people watched and applauded and the air was filled with the sweet smell released by the burning of spices in the streets. This was how they celebrated a victory. In the same way, Christians are called to spiritual warfare and are triumphantly led by God in Christ, and it is through him that God spreads everywhere the "fragrance" of the knowledge of Christ.

Read 2 Corinthians 2:16

The sweet fragrance Paul is speaking of here is the aroma of the Gospel released in the world through Christian testimony. But it is received differently by two ultimate categories of mankind: those being saved and those who are perishing. To the perishing, a Christian's testimony is the smell of death because in rejecting the life-giving grace of God, the unbelievers are choosing death for themselves. But to those who welcome the Gospel of God's grace, Christians with their testimony are the fragrance of life.

Our sense of smell varies. Some people love to smell seafood cooking, others can't stand the smell. Some like the smell of fried liver, others detest it. How does the gospel smell to you? Is it the sweet fragrance of life or the stench of death? It didn't matter to Paul where he preached as long as God was glorified. Some were converted, some were condemned. We need to faithfully present the gospel wherever we have the God-given opportunity to do so.

Read 2 Corinthians 2:17

Here Paul is referring to the false teachers who had infiltrated the Corinthian church. They were insincere, self-sufficient, boastful, and very persuasive. Their chief interest was taking money from gullible church members. Paul, by contrast, had preached the gospel sincerely and free of charge, taking care not to be a financial burden to the Corinthian believers.

Let us speak to others "with sincerity, like men sent from God."

Some of the things we learn from this chapter:
1. local churches have a responsibility to discipline members who sin;
2. discipline is not in the hands of one man, but is the responsibility of the congregation—neither the deacons or pastor have final authority, but the congregation (not even Paul felt he had that authority);
3. the purpose of discipline should be to restore the offending person-- to bring the offender to repentance and back into the service of the church;
4. repentance should be followed by forgiveness and restoration;
5. if we are led by the Spirit, there are times we may have to change our plans;
6. we should not consider every opportunity to be a calling from God;
7. wrong handling of discipline can be turned by Satan to his advantage. (see vs. 11—repentance must be followed quickly by forgiveness and restoration "lest Satan should get an advantage of us: for we are not ignorant of his devices.")

Satan can take advantage of a disciplinary action within a church:
- He would first tempt the believer to sin, ruining his life and testimony;
- Then he would tempt him to think he is hopeless;
- He would tempt the church to overlook the sin and coddle the sinful members, or cause them to act harshly and discipline with a vengeance;
- Then he would tempt the one who was disciplined to become bitter and resentful.
- If he repents, Satan will tempt the church to withhold forgiveness.

2 Corinthians – Chapter 3

Paul has been asked by the Corinthian church to provide to them a letter of commendation.

Read 2 Corinthians 3:1-2

When applying for a job, the application usually includes a section to give names of people who can give the company a reference about the applicant. Even a church looking for a new pastor, minister, preacher, or other such leader of the church, will want some type of recommendation. Any church would be foolish not to require certain credentials from a possible leader.

Paul understood this concept because he had given letters of recommendation before.

Read Romans 16:1

Note: The word *deacon* refers here to a Christian designated to serve with the overseers/elders of the church in a variety of ways.

Paul is giving a letter of recommendation for Phoebe so the church in Rome will know she is a true servant of the Lord and not a false prophetess.

Read 1 Corinthians 16:3

Here Paul promises letters of introduction to those who are approved by the Church so there will be no mistaking them for false teachers.

But now the Church in Corinth is asking Paul for his credentials. They are a church and Paul is a preacher, so why is this a problem? Because these people KNOW Paul. In fact, he is the founding pastor of their church! They would be the ones who would normally give others a recommendation for him. So this was an insult to Paul for them to question him in this way. They were Christians because of him; he preached the gospel to them and taught them about Christ.

But after Paul left Corinth, impostors came into the church claiming to be teachers of God's truth. They brought with them forged letters of recommendation to authenticate their authority.

Paul was very aware that everything he wrote or said was liable to be twisted and used against him by the false teachers in Corinth. So he explains to them that they, the members of the Church, are his recommendation because of the power of the gospel that was demonstrated by their transformed lives. Paul had no written letters of commendation, but explains his letters are in the form of the people themselves—they are saints because of him.

In the King James translation, verse 2 reads *"Ye are our epistle."* Think of it this way: Christ was the Writer; Paul was the instrument or pen; the Holy Spirit was the ink; and the heart of the believer was the paper.

Even today, we are living letters of Christ. Think of yourself as a letter of recommendation for Christ. Is that what people see in you? Would they feel good about placing Christ into their lives on your recommendation?

A letter of recommendation must be legible if it is to be read. It should be consistent and logical, or it will be meaningless to the reader. Above all, a letter should express the writer's thoughts and personality.

YOU are Christ's letter, a letter which is "known and read of all men." We, as Christians, don't have a choice as to whether we wish to be epistles of Christ. We are—so how do people read you?

> *"We are the only Bible the careless world will read,*
> *We are the sinner's gospel, We are the scoffer's creed,*
> *We are the Lord's last message, Given in deed and word,*
> *What if the type is crooked? What if the print is blurred?"*
> *...By Annie Johnson Flint*

Read 2 Corinthians 3:3

Paul says they are better than mere ink on paper or tablets of stone (referring to the old law delivered to Moses on stone tablets). Their stamp of approval is in their hearts in the form of the Spirit, which is more permanent.

Read Proverbs 3:3

Read Jeremiah 31:33

Ink fades and may easily be deleted or blocked out since it is no more than an inanimate fluid. But the Spirit of the Living God is Himself life and therefore life-giving, and the life He gives is eternal and without defect.

Read 2 Corinthians 3:4-5

Back in 2 Corinthians 2:16, Paul asks the question "who is equal to such a task?" Here is where he answers his own question. Our confidence comes from God through Christ. Then he goes on to give God all the credit for his accomplishments. The false teachers boasted of their own power and prestige.

Read John 15:5

Paul recognized this fact. He expressed his humility before God. No one can carry out the responsibilities of God's calling in his or her own strength. Without the Holy Spirit, our natural talent can carry us only so far. We need the character and special strength only God can give as we witness for Christ.

Read 2 Corinthians 3:6

Note: "Ministers" here refers to anyone serving Christ. "New covenant" refers to the new covenant given to His followers by Christ.

Read 1 Timothy 4:6

Read Luke 22:20

What does he mean when he says "the letter kills"?

Read Romans 7:6

The old law, which was written, only condemns us to death. It had no power to save us. It was impossible for man to obey all the laws and therefore all men were condemned. But, through Christ's sacrifice, the Spirit gives us eternal life.

Read John 6:63

The law was given to help man realize their sinfulness, but it did not give life. The moral law, including the Ten Commandments, still points out sin and show us how to obey God, but forgiveness comes only through the grace and mercy of Christ.

The Spirit gives life.

Read 2 Corinthians 3:7-11

What Paul is saying in his roundabout way is this: If the Law of Moses was so glorious the Israelites couldn't look upon his face, and that glory faded with time, imagine how much more glorious is this new ministry of the Spirit, which brings righteousness and will last forever.

Paul makes it clear the old covenant of the Law of Moses was NOT evil or bad, but was glorious in its own way because it came from God.

Read Romans 7:12, 22

Evil exists in the hearts and deeds of people who bring upon themselves the condemnation of the law and the penalty of death by breaking the laws God gave. By having the laws written on stone tablets, there was still no way for those tablets to purge away that evil from man.

The Law was not permanent. God never intended it to be.

Read Galatians 3:19, 24-25

"Transitory" means "brief" or "fleeting." Paul is saying the "glory" that shone in the face of Moses when he descended Mt. Sinai, the brilliant light that surrounded him, eventually faded. This is also paralleled by the fact that the Law also eventually faded. It was given as a 'temporary' fix—until the Lord, our Savior, could come. So the old covenant was superseded by the permanent and much more glorious radiance of the new covenant.

Let's look at it this way: When you get up at 5:00 in the morning, you must turn on a light to see. But as the sun rises, the light bulb is no longer needed. In fact, the sun shines so bright the light bulb looks dim. There is no electric light in the world that can outshine the sun. In the same way, the glory of the gospel of grace outshines the glory associated with Moses' face.

Read 2 Corinthians 3:12-13

Read Exodus 34:33-35

Paul reveals to us why Moses veiled his face. Moses didn't want the Israelites to witness the fading of the glory. Whenever he entered the Lord's presence, the radiance became strong again, but diminished with time until he visited the Lord again. So he covered his face to keep them from seeing it fade.

Read 2 Corinthians 3:14-16

What Paul is saying here is that those who continue to live by the old law are blinded to God's Word.

Note: The word used here for "blinded" literally means "to harden, to make like stone."

Their minds are not open to the new covenant; therefore it's as if the veil is still there hiding the Light of Truth. Only through Christ can the veil be stripped away so they will understand. Whenever someone turns to the Lord, the veil is lifted and their minds are opened so they can understand God's Word. Without the veil, we can be like mirrors reflecting God's glory.

Read 2 Corinthians 3:17

Back in verse 6, it says "the Spirit gives life." Now Paul says "the Lord is the Spirit"—if we link these together we now have "the Lord is the Spirit and the Spirit gives life." Only by turning to the Lord can the condemnation and the sentence of death pronounced by the old law be annulled and replaced by the life-giving grace of the new covenant.

The law caused people to get tied up in rules and ceremonies. Being free from the law through our trust in Christ frees us from that burden. We are loved, accepted, forgiven, and freed to live for Him.

Read Romans 8:1

Read 2 Corinthians 3:18

Contemplate means "to reflect." We, as Christians, should be an unveiled light, reflecting God's glory. As we draw closer to God through His Word and through our relationship with Him, we grow increasingly like Him by living more pure and spiritual lives rather than earthly, sinful lives. His glory will shine from us. Becoming Christ-like is a progressive experience and should be our goal in life.

The Greek word used here, which was translated as "transformed," is the basis of our English word "metamorphosis." The Greek word's *opposite* is "conformed." "Transformed" means a change from within. "Conformed" means a change due to external pressures. External forces will not change a caterpillar into a butterfly. Only innate characteristics will cause the change. In the same way, we are not to allow the worldly pressures to cause us to "act like" Christians because it's what we think we should do, but we are to be transformed from within ourselves.

Read Hebrews 1:3

As Christians, we are being gradually transformed into the likeness of Christ as we grow in the knowledge and glory of The Word. By meeting with Him on a daily basis, the glow of His glory should stay with us. It is only as we read His Word that we can see Him; and the more we see Him, the more we become like Him.

F.A.C.T.S.

Many of us make resolutions at the beginning of a new year, but resolutions can be made any time. What about Christ do you want people to 'read' in you? Let's all make a resolution to be a glowing recommendation for Christ, in the way we live and the way others see us and Christ within us.

2 Corinthians – Chapter 4

Read 2 Corinthians 4:1

The ministry Paul is speaking of here is the new covenant rather than the old covenant of the law.

Read 2 Corinthians 4:2

Paul is referring to the false teachers who invaded the church in Corinth. He renounces their secret, shameful, and deceptive ways. He's reminding the Christians in Corinth he never deceived them or distorted God's message, but rather told them the plain and simple truth.

Read 2 Corinthians 4:3

For those who have accepted Christ, the message he taught them was easily understood. But for those who had not accepted Christ, their minds couldn't comprehend what he taught. Their minds were 'veiled' as discussed in chapter 3. The unbeliever is blinded from the light of the gospel. The fact that a blind man cannot see the sun doesn't diminish the brilliance of its light. The same is true with the gospel. Even if the unbeliever cannot see the truth doesn't make it untrue.

Read 1 Corinthians 2:14

Read 2 Corinthians 4:4

"The god of this age" refers to Satan. His work is to deceive. The allure of money, power, and other pleasures blinds people to the light of the gospel of Christ. All who reject Christ, preferring their own pursuits, have unknowingly chosen to make Satan their god. Satan is the unseen power behind all unbelief and ungodliness.

"This age" refers to the time prior to the age of eternal life when Satan shall be purged along with anything that defiles God's creation.

Read 2 Corinthians 4:5

The false teachers had inflated egos, fixated on their own self-importance. Paul explains he never felt important, but what was important was his message of Christ. People must be introduced to Christ, not us. We must be sure to tell people about what Christ has done, not brag about what we've done or are doing in His name.

Being a follower of Christ means serving others, even when they do not measure up to our expectations. Serving people requires a sacrifice of time and personal desires. Paul willingly served the Corinthian church even though they must have deeply disappointed him at times.

Read 2 Corinthians 4:6

"Let light shine out of darkness." This is what God said at the creation in Genesis 1:3, but it also pertains to Christians because the darkness of sin is ousted by the light of the gospel.

"The light of the knowledge of God's glory."

Read John 1:14

The light shining in Paul's heart is due to the knowledge of the glory of God, which was shown to him through Christ who came from the glorious presence of God in heaven itself.

Have you ever asked yourself, or maybe even said out loud, "Why don't more people respond to the gospel message and accept Christ?" In asking this question, we're assuming the message has been properly presented to them.

Read Romans 10:12-17

For someone to respond to the gospel message, THE WORD must be given in a clear and understandable manner; it must be bathed in prayer; and the lives of those presenting the message must reflect what they say. No one will trust or believe a hypocrite.

Even Paul struggled with this reality. He had received this glorious ministry from the Lord, a message bringing life and righteousness, liberty and glory. He didn't feel deserving of being the messenger, not only because he felt inadequate as most of us do today, but because he had been a persecutor of Christians prior to his transformation. But God had shown him mercy and forgiven him, giving him this important task to teach others about Jesus.

It isn't our past that portrays us, but our present. We can be forgiven for past mistakes. God's grace is sufficient. But we cannot preach one thing while living another.

So many times we try to witness, yet we fall short of knowing what to say. We walk away thinking, "if only I had said this when he said that."

Paul faced a lot of opposition and false teachers, yet he never gave up. He continued to preach the gospel openly and faithfully. He was never ashamed of how he preached.

He knew what he was talking about. His information came straight from the Lord, yet even he was unable to convince a lot of people. So we shouldn't be discouraged when we fall short with our limited knowledge. That's not to say we shouldn't strive to learn more so we can be more confident in our attempts to spread the gospel, but we can't let our failures cause us to quit trying.

Salvation is an act of God, not of man. It is our job to prayerfully and carefully present the gospel to lost souls. But we can't make them believe. God has to initiate the work of salvation.

Also, we must present God's Word truthfully. When we tell people about Christ, we must be careful not to distort the message to please our audience. Remember, God is in that audience, listening to every word we say.

Read 2 Corinthians 4:7

Clay jars were used to conceal precious treasure because they were so ordinary they didn't draw attention to themselves and their precious contents. In the same way, our grandmothers used a tin can to stash their extra cash. Paul is comparing himself to the clay jars. He sees himself as plain and unworthy, and yet he has within him this wonderful treasure of a message from God. Because he sees himself as unimportant and frail, they can know the powerful message is from God and not from Paul.

Read 1 Corinthians 1:26-29

Throughout the scriptures, God used the most humble and meek people to deliver His messages. Even the disciples Christ chose to follow Him were among the most undesirable men of that day. By using people with little influence, God is making sure it is evident the power of the message is from Him, not the messenger. The emphasis remains on God and what He can do.

Read 2 Corinthians 4:8-9

Paul says although they are being bombarded from all sides, it has not crushed their resolve. Although sometimes at a loss for understanding, they are not hopeless. Although they are being persecuted, they have not been abandoned by God. And although they've been knocked down, they have not been knocked out.

So even when it appears Satan is winning the battle, God is faithful and gives us strength to endure. All of our humiliations and trials are opportunities for Christ to demonstrate his power and presence through us.

Read 2 Corinthians 4:10-12

Paul is saying because he has suffered many hardships and been persecuted because of his preaching the gospel of Christ, he shares in the suffering of Christ.

Read 2 Corinthians 1:5

Read Romans 8:17

In verse 12, the "life is at work in you" refers to Christ's resurrection which is what the gospel message is all about.

Suffering relates to salvation the same as labor pains relates to the birth of a child. The Bible is full of stories where the servant suffers, but souls are saved. So if you are being taunted or are suffering because you are a Christian, remember it is through this that someone may come to Christ.

Read 2 Corinthians 4:13-15

The quote in verse 13 is from the scripture found in Psalm 116:10. True belief and faith leads to testimony, which is why Paul tirelessly labored and traveled to take the gospel message to others.

As long as God has a job for you to do, nothing can stop it from happening as long as you're willing. Satan will try to deter you from witnessing by using your weaknesses, but God can give us the resolve to continue to be faithful and some will be saved because of it. Remember the glory must go to God. It is HIS power that saves. We are a plain container in which His treasure of The Word can be stored.

Read 2 Corinthians 4:16-17

Here Paul goes back to his original thought started in verse 1. Because he knows all his suffering is for God's glory, for all the reasons he has written here, he will not be discouraged.

Paul had suffered a lot since his conversion, beginning immediately after he accepted Christ and continuing for over thirty years. They plotted to kill him in Damascus and in Jerusalem, drove him out of Antioch, attempted to stone him in Iconium, stoned him and left him for dead in Lystra, beat him with rods in Philippi and put him in stocks. In Thessalonica, the Jews and others tried to mob him. They drove him out of Berea, plotted against him in Corinth and almost killed him in Ephesus. Shortly after writing the 2 Corinthians letter, they again plotted his death in Corinth, and they would have killed him in Jerusalem if the Roman soldiers had not intervened. Then he was imprisoned in Caesarea for two years, and two more in Rome. And these are only the incidents that are recorded. There were probably many other unrecorded beatings, imprisonments, shipwrecks, and attempts on his life.

In verse 16, he says his mortal body is "wasting away" because of the hardships he has been through.

They are "being renewed" because of the inextinguishable flame of the truth of the resurrection burning within them giving them a cheerful heart. His message here is the inward renewal of his soul through Christ overcomes the outward destruction of his physical body due to the hardships he's had to endure, and ultimately will overcome even death itself. In the light of eternity, the Christians difficulties, whatever they may be, diminish in importance. By comparison, eternal glory is far greater than all the suffering one might face in this life.

Read 2 Corinthians 4:18

The experiences we face in this present life, which often seem painful and puzzling, are what's apparent to us as Christians. But these are merely a temporary and fleeting phenomena. To continue fixating our thoughts on these things would cause us to lose heart, or become depressed. But if we keep focused on the unseen realities of eternity, we will obtain a lasting peace. We need to be like athletes and focus on the finish line, ignoring the discomfort as we strive to reach it. No matter what happens in this life, we have the assurance of eternal life, when all suffering will end and "all sorrow will flee away" as we're told in Isaiah 35:10.

Have you ever wondered what you would do if faced with the choice of dying for Christ or denying Him and keeping your life? In today's world, this question is becoming an increasing possibility. Look at what happened at Columbine. The shooters asked the teen-age girl if she believed in Jesus Christ and she firmly acknowledged she did and was immediately shot to death. The possibility of facing death for our faith has become a reality in our lives.

F.A.C.T.S.

What is faith?

Read Hebrews 11:1, 26-27

The things of God may be invisible, but that doesn't mean they are any less real.

Read Hebrews 12:2-3

How can we encourage other Christians who are confused or bogged down by the cares of this life?

Paul's message is not to lose hope.

Problems and human limitations provide several benefits:
1. They remind us of Christ's suffering for us;
2. They keep us from pride;
3. They cause us to look beyond this brief life;
4. They prove our faith to others;
5. They give God the opportunity to demonstrate His power

So view your troubles as opportunities.

Knowing we will live forever with God in a place without sin and suffering can help us live above the pain we face in this life.

2 Corinthians – Chapter 5

Paul continues the message he started in 2 Corinthians 4:18 regarding temporary vs. permanent.

Read 2 Corinthians 4:18

Read 2 Corinthians 5:1

"earthly tent we live in" is our present body. A tent is a temporary and flimsy dwelling just as our bodies are frail and vulnerable and wasting away.

"a building from God, an eternal house in heaven" will be a solid structure that is permanent, not temporary.

This is one of the *"unseen"* things Paul spoke of in 4:18.

"not built by human hands," means our new structure will be made by God, therefore perfect and permanent.

It is only natural Paul would choose a tent as a metaphor since he was a tent-maker. Notice he distinctly separates the "real person" from the body. The tent is "dissolved" *(from the Greek word meaning "dismantled" or "to take down")*. But the real person *(or the soul)* continues on.

Consider how much money is spent on trying to prolong the life of our physical bodies, which are temporary. Millions is spent in an attempt to make us look better, have healthier bodies, and constantly "patching" our tents. This is not wrong, because we should take good care of this temporary dwelling God has entrusted in our care. But compare that to what little time, effort, and money we spend on the only part of us that will survive, our soul. It is given very little attention.

Read 1 John 3:2

Read Philippians 3:20-21

So we don't really know what these new bodies will be like, but we know we will be in the likeness of Christ, free from disease, distress, death and decay. And we will be in God's presence.

Read 2 Corinthians 5:2-4

"we groan" because we long for our perfect dwelling in heaven and to be rid of this temporary earthly *"tent."* At death, between the time of our earthly life and our eternal life in heaven, there is a brief interval of time when we will be *"naked"* – without earthly or heavenly bodies. We will depart from our frail earthly body and then be clothed in our permanent heavenly dwelling.

"mortal may be swallowed up by life" – Anything mortal is going to die eventually. So when we think of losing this earthly body, we think of death. But Paul points out we are NOT swallowed up by death, but by life—because of the resurrection.

Read Proverbs 1:12

In the Old Testament, death and the grave was thought of as the great swallower. Life in the form of our eternal spiritual life will consume and overcome our mortal existence.

Read 2 Corinthians 5:5

When Christ arose, he sent the Holy Spirit. This is a deposit on the promise of our eventual total transformation to be with, and like, Christ when our time comes to enter death's door.

Read 2 Corinthians 5:6-8

As long as we are 'at home' in our earthly 'tent dwelling', we are separated from the Lord.

Look at it this way. We are on a journey. We have left our home and are traveling. During our travels we are living in a tent, which is a temporary shelter. Since our journey is a long one, our tent becomes more and more shabby and deteriorated. But when we finally end our journey, we will return home to our stable permanent dwelling.

Now while we're away from home, we yearn to get back to our comfortable and warm home. But we continue on because we have faith our home will be waiting for us upon our return. Even though we can't see it at the moment, we have faith in it being there. For those who are in Christ, death is simply a prelude to eternal life with God. We will continue to live. This hope gives us the confidence and inspiration to faithfully serve Him.

Read 2 Corinthians 5:9-10

Read Philippians 1:23

There is a brief time (a twinkling of an eye) between death and resurrection when we are disembodied, but we are home with our Lord, which is preferable to being in our 'earthly tent'.

Paul is clearly telling us when we die, we immediately go to be in God's presence. There is no purgatory or waiting room. We do not remain in the grave until an appointed time. To be absent from the body is to be with the Lord.

We will appear before the judgment seat, but not to judge whether we can go to heaven or hell. Christians already know they will be in heaven with Christ, but we will be judged on what we have done with our lives as Christians.

The word "appear" here does not only imply being present. But it also means things will be brought to light.

Read 1 Corinthians 3:11-15

So although our bodies are wasting away and we know we are saved and going to heaven for eternity, we are still responsible for our actions while still in this body.

Sin is not mentioned here because, as Christians, our sins have been washed away. They are no longer remembered. We will not be judged concerning our sins. But God will be more concerned about how we spent our time as Christians; whether we were fruitful or not in bringing others to Christ and helping our fellow Christians. We will be appearing before Christ as "servants," not as "sinners."

Read Hebrews 10:17

What about unconfessed sins? Will those be judged then? No. They are dealt with here on earth as God deals with us as His children. The question of sin is already settled for those within the Church.

Read Hebrews 12:5-11

Remember, Paul is speaking to Christians in this letter. Non-Christians will be judged for rejecting Christ and for their sins as we are told in Romans 2:5-16.

Our motives will also be judged. What we do is important, but why we do it will be more important.

Read 1 Corinthians 4:5

Works performed for self-glorification will not receive rewards. As Christ said in Matthew 6:2, "they have their reward already."

The quality of our works will be judged.

Read 1 Corinthians 3:13

This should re-assure us that quality is more important than quantity. So although all of us do not have the same opportunities and gifts, all are judged by the same standard—by our faithfulness to the task. Equal faithfulness will bring equal reward.

There will be crowns of glory for all kinds of things. There are specific crowns for peace keepers, preachers, soul-winners, those who are persecuted, and for those who look forward to His appearing.

Read 2 Timothy 4:8

But the greatest reward will be to have Christ smile and say to us "Well done, you good and faithful servant." Just imagine!

Read 2 Corinthians 5:11-12

Paul is defending his position again against the false teachers who have infiltrated the Church in Corinth. Paul reminds them he knows what it is to fear the Lord. He says God knows he is an apostle, and he hopes the people in the Church can recognize that fact also. In verse 12 he says the false teachers are those who take pride in what is seen rather than in what is in the heart. They are full of pretense and their concern is with money and popularity and self-importance rather than things of the spirit. We can weed out the "false teachers" by determining their motivation. If they are more concerned about themselves than about Christ, avoid them.

Read 2 Corinthians 5:13-15

Paul has been accused of being a crazy religious fanatic, but he says if that's what they want to believe, then so be it. This entire letter stresses how willing he is to endure affliction for the Gospel. Paul never used any kind of trickery or sensationalism when he taught the gospel to the people in Corinth. He was always sincere and sensible, never eccentric.

If he appears obsessed or too consumed by his message, it is because of Christ's love as shown in His death for all. He is not speaking literally about all of mankind, but is referring to all of those within the Church who have accepted Christ as Lord and Savior. Because Christ died for all, those of us who now claim life over death because of our belief in Him, should no longer live for ourselves, but for Christ.

Read 2 Corinthians 5:16

If we are living for Christ, we no longer see things from a worldly point of view.

"we once regarded Christ in this way": Paul explains that before his conversion, he viewed Jesus in a worldly way, seeing Him as just a man.

Read 2 Corinthians 5:17

"in Christ": united with Christ through faith in Him and commitment to Him. Anyone who is in Christ is a new creation.

"new creation": our redemption in Christ fulfills and restores God's original purposes of our creation—to be companions with Him and walk with Him. He didn't create us to be separated from Him, but only through sin were we separated because God couldn't be a part of sin. When we come to Christ, we are cleansed of sin and can be united with Him, the creator of all things. At conversion, we are not merely turning over a new leaf; we are not reformed, rehabilitated, or reeducated—we are "reborn", or re-created, living in union with Christ.

Read Hebrews 1:2

Read 2 Corinthians 5:18-19

God, because of His love for us, sent Christ so we could be redeemed. But it didn't stop there. He also gave us a job to do in return. He gave us this ministry to spread the message. We should see this as a privilege to serve God, who has given us so much, not as a chore to be dreaded.

Paul uses the word "reconciled." Think about this word for a minute. When we reconcile, we come back together. For instance, if we are separated or divorced from each other and we reconcile, we have ironed out our differences and come back together in like mindedness. This is what Paul is speaking about. God has brought us BACK to Him by blotting out our sins and making us righteous so we can walk with Him and in His presence. So our ministry is called "a ministry of reconciliation" because we are to encourage others to become reconciled with God.

Read 2 Corinthians 5:20-21

An ambassador is a representative, so we are to represent Christ. Christ was righteous and perfect, completely without sin. But when He was crucified, He took upon Him all of our sins and died a painful death, becoming a sin offering for us. For that brief moment, he was separated from God because of that sin.

When we accept Christ, we complete an exchange. At His crucifixion, our sin was poured into Christ. At our conversion, Christ's righteousness is poured into us. This is what the phrase "atonement for sin" means. In the world's view, bartering means trading something of worth for something else of equal value. But God offers to trade His righteousness (something of immeasurable worth) for our sin (something completely worthless).

We should be so grateful for this kindness God has given us that we proudly fulfill our commission as Christ's ambassadors by sharing the Gospel and showing others how they can be reconciled with God.

2 Corinthians – Chapter 6

Paul reminds us not to take God's grace for granted. He calls us God's "co-workers," not His employees or servants. His CO-WORKERS! I don't know about you, but it is difficult for me to see myself on the same level as God, as His fellow worker or partner. To know God thinks of us that way is very humbling, yet empowering at the same time.

Read 2 Corinthians 6:1-2

If we continue to live for ourselves rather than for Christ, then we have received God's grace in vain. Paul quotes Isaiah 49:8, informing the Corinthians the "day of salvation" spoken of in the scriptures is now.

Every saving act God performed in the history of Israel finds fulfillment in this age of grace. God told Israel He heard them, and in the day of salvation He'd help them. The "day of salvation" would be later, after the coming of Christ.

Read 2 Corinthians 1:20

All the promises God made in the Old Testament were fulfilled through the coming of Christ. It is because of

Christ we can say "so be it," which is what "Amen" means.

Read John 8:56

Jesus told the Jews Abraham rejoiced when Jesus left Heaven and came to earth to fulfill the promise made to him. Although Abraham died before he saw the promises God had made to him fulfilled, he did see it happen—and he rejoiced.

Read Hebrews 11:13

The writer of Hebrews explains how the descendants of Abraham, who were as numerous as the stars in the sky, were living by faith when they died. They did not receive the things promised them in their lifetime on earth, but they DID see them and welcome them from a distance. They knew they were not of this earth, yet they were able to watch Christ fulfill the promise made to Abraham and rejoice in it.

Those who lived prior to Christ's coming, those who believed in the Old Testament teachings, saw and welcomed the fulfillment of God's promises from a distance.

Read 2 Corinthians 6:3-10

Paul is concerned about keeping his testimony pure by keeping his life pure. He doesn't want to do anything to discourage others from hearing and accepting the message about Christ. We should be as diligent in our daily lives. Remember, in the course of your day, there are many non-Christians observing you. Don't allow your actions be another person's excuse for rejecting Christ.

Verses 4-5 describe the testing of a Christian worker; 6-7 describe characteristics of a Christian worker; 8-10 contain 9 contradictions which are true about a Christian worker.

In verse 10, Paul reminds us true wealth does not come from earthly possessions, but from being "rich in Godly things."

Read Luke 12:20-21

Read Ephesians 3:8

Read Philippians 4:19

What are these riches?

Read Colossians 2:2-3

Read 2 Corinthians 6:11-13

Paul has always loved the Christians in Corinth and been completely open and honest with them. But in return, they have started believing the false teachings of the fake apostles who have entered their church. They've been telling them Paul is the fake and doesn't really love them. So here Paul explains he does love them, just as he would his own children, and asks for their loyalty.

Read 2 Corinthians 6:14-15

Belial – Original Greek was Beliar, a variant of Belial, a Hebrew term used for Satan.

Paul is obviously speaking to the church about allowing non-believers in their midst and allowing them to infiltrate the teachings of the church. But this can also apply to us when choosing friends and spouses.

Paul has pre-qualified this statement back in 1 Corinthians 5:9-12.

Read 1 Corinthians 5:9-12

Paul is not suggesting we isolate ourselves from everyone who is sinful. But he is telling us not to allow them to infiltrate the Church.

In fact Paul goes as far as to tell us NOT to isolate ourselves from sinners—even in our families.

Read 1 Corinthians 7:12-13

If we isolate ourselves, we can't be fruitful in bringing others to Christ. But don't allow those who are not saved to influence the way we live and believe.

Read 2 Corinthians 6:16-17

There can be no compromise within the church to appease those who don't believe as we do. The Corinthian Church had turned away from idolatry in favor of the Gospel of Christ. Now they are accepting some of the idol worshippers among them. Paul is warning them against reverting back to their old ways.

He's not talking about the fact that they allow these people in the building. The Church he's speaking of here is the people, the living stones, the believers. It is all important they don't form defiling and unholy alliances that will cause them to turn from, or get distracted from, the teachings of Christ.

"As God has said": this is quoting Leviticus 26:12; Jeremiah 32:38; & Ezekiel 37:27

Verse 17 was taken from Isaiah 52:11 and Ezekiel 20:34,41.

Paul says we should separate ourselves in that we must not allow the sinful nature of those around us to infiltrate and influence our lives. We need to stand strong and faithful in the Lord. We should live among others in this world so we can witness to them, but we should stand apart by not joining in their sinful and worldly ways.

Read 2 Corinthians 6:18

This quote was taken from 2 Samuel 7:14 & 7:8. God has adopted us into His family as His children and brothers and sisters to Christ Jesus. What a wonderful and glorious family we have!

2 Corinthians – Chapter 7

In this chapter, Paul continues the theme he started at the end of chapter 6.

Read 2 Corinthians 7:1

He tells us to turn away from anything contaminating our lives—both physical and spiritual—anything distracting us from our reverence of God.

"Perfecting holiness" means to have nothing whatsoever to do with anything unGodly—such as paganism, which was a huge problem during that time.

Read 2 Corinthians 7:2-4

It's implied here once again that Paul had been accused by the false teachers of being unjust, destructive and fraudulent—the very things those teachers were guilty of being.

Paul asks the Corinthians for their love and devotion. Then he goes on to tell them how much they mean to him. Paul was pleading with them because he has been so hurt by their turning away from him to follow the false teachers who have entered the church. He loved them so much and couldn't understand how they could turn on him like this.

Paul sometimes speaks about how he "had no rest." The word "rest" was sometimes used to mean a bow being unstrung or the release of tension of the strings of a musical instrument. So unrest would have depicted a tightly strung bow or instrument—meaning lots of tension! Part of Paul's tension was due to the sin infiltrating the Corinthian church.

But in verse 4, Paul talks about how joyful he is and how much confidence he has in them.

Read 2 Corinthians 7:5-7

Paul sent Timothy earlier, as we studied in 1 Corinthians, but Timothy was timid and not suited for the stern discipline required by the situation in Corinth. Paul had heard how the people had turned on him, so he chose Titus to go to them and deliver another letter. This letter was written between the letter we know as 1 Corinthians and the one we have as 2 Corinthians, but must have been lost. We do not have a record of it other than Paul mentioning it in chapter 2, verse 3. Titus was more capable of conveying the stern message Paul needed delivered.

The person or people who had started the trouble in the church, the false teachers, were probably very influential. They had persisted in their sin and led an open revolt against Paul, swaying some of the leaders in the church. But upon the arrival of Titus, with Paul's letter, the Church was brought back into line, and the trouble makers had been humiliated and removed. This was part of the good news Titus had reported to Paul.

Here Paul refers back to when he went to Macedonia looking for Titus and how Titus had helped him by giving him the good news and telling him about their love for him. He told Paul they still loved and respected him after all. This made Paul happy. They had received his second letter and actually heeded his warnings.

Titus also told him of the deep sorrow the people in the Church of Corinth felt because of the grief they had caused Paul.

Read 2 Corinthians 7:8-9

Paul explains how, although he didn't enjoy reprimanding them, he was glad he wrote the letter, bringing them to repentance. So although his letter may have hurt them at the time, it brought about the results God had intended and they were not harmed by their sorrow, but rather redeemed by their repentance. Discipline isn't a pleasant task, but sometimes it produces wonderful results.

Read Hebrews 12:11

We learn from this chapter in 2 Corinthians, as with most of Paul's writings, he believes in being firm against the enemies of the gospel, uncompromising of the truth; yet he was sensitive and compassionate toward the people in the church. Paul had a big heart for people.

Read 2 Corinthians 7:10-12

Godly sorrow is when we feel we have offended God. This kind of sorrow brings about repentance, which in turn leads to salvation. Once you have salvation, you should no longer regret the sorrow that got you there, but rejoice in it. But sin can cause you worldly sorrow (such as loss of your job, your family, friends, health, etc.) This kind of sorrow causes death. Worldly sorrow may bring about remorse and even tears, but stops short of repentance. Without repentance, you reap the wages of sin—which is death. Godly sorrow is not being sorrowful for the consequences of the sin, but sorry for the sin itself. Regret is not repentance. Regret usually happens because you're sorry you got caught—or had to pay the consequences. Repentance is being remorseful for committing the sin and causes a change in how you approach things in the future.

(Quoted from Life Application Bible) "Rather than become defensive and too proud to admit when we have done wrong, we need to accept correction as a tool for growth and do all we can to correct those problems that have been pointed out to us."

"Regret" causes desperation. "Repentance" gives us peace of mind.

Because of Paul showing them where they were going wrong, they were able to correct it and now are intense about their beliefs again and eager to make things right again. They are now alarmed by their lack of diligence and long to worship God more earnestly. So even though his letter was harsh, it wasn't to accuse them of any wrongdoing, but to show them how devoted they were. Paul says he knew they were good people and were devoted to their beliefs, but they had become confused and just needed to be straightened out.

Read 2 Corinthians 7:13-16

Paul had bragged to Titus about what terrific people the Corinthians were and is glad they had received him well and treated him with respect when Titus went to see them. Titus' spirits were lifted by being with them and it had proven Paul to be right about them. If they had treated Titus with a cold shoulder, Paul would have been embarrassed about bragging on them so much. But they had made him proud of them and he says he has complete confidence in them.

Paul's apprehension and anxiety had been replaced by rejoicing and reassurance.

If your pastor were to write a letter concerning your obedience to the Word or his confidence in you, would it be a letter of rejoicing or of discouragement?

F.A.C.T.S.

One thing that helped relieve Paul's tension was his friend Titus. He was full of joy when he was visited by Titus. Then Titus brought him such good news about the Corinthians turning away from their sin, which made Paul even happier. Let's not overlook the importance of our friends during times when we are tense and could use some good news. Our Christian friends are God's answer to our headaches in life.

2 Corinthians – Chapter 8

As we studied in 1 Corinthians 16, Paul set up a system to collect donations from all of the churches to be taken to the church in Jerusalem for the poor saints. Jewish Christians near Jerusalem were reportedly on the verge of starvation. This letter was written about a year later, according to verse 10 in this chapter. When he wrote this letter, he was visiting the churches in Macedonia, where he fled to after the riots in Ephesus as described in Acts 19.

He wanted the other churches to know how faithful the Macedonian churches had been. Paul saw this as an opportunity for Gentile Christians to reach out in compassion and demonstrate their spiritual unity with Jewish Christians.

Read 2 Corinthians 8:1-5

The Macedonian churches had entered into giving to the poor wholeheartedly. Even the very poor were giving generously, even beyond what they could afford. They not only gave what they could for the poor, but wanted to give to Paul and his companions to help them in their journeys.

Read 2 Corinthians 8:6-7

The churches had found joy in giving, so Paul was encouraged to teach the grace of giving to the Corinthian churches so they might also share in this joyfulness. So Paul sent Titus with this letter to the churches in Corinth. He says that he knows how much they desire to please God. They are so full of faith, eloquent in speech, and possess so much knowledge. Because of this, they should be willing to excel in the grace of giving to others.

Read 2 Corinthians 8:8-9

Paul explains that this is not a commandment, but something they should do to show their love. He reminds them how Jesus set the example by leaving His glorified place in Heaven to come to earth where He was no more than an ordinary man so that He could show us how we should live. He did this for our sake, so we should pay it forward.

Read 2 Corinthians 8:10-12

A year prior to this letter, the churches in Corinth had given willingly to help the poor as Paul had asked. He asks them to continue this practice. He does not ask them to give beyond their means. He asked them to willingly give according to what they had. He stresses how it is important to give willingly. If it is given grudgingly, God does not accept it. Only a gift out of love is acknowledged by God.

Read 2 Corinthians 8:13-15

Paul quotes the Old Testament scripture found in Exodus 16:18, which explains the principle of sharing with others so everyone can be equal. The idea was if you have more than you need, you give to those who have little. In return, when their harvest is more abundant and you are need, they can return the favor. This is a principle from God and hasn't changed since the beginning of time. Hording for our future while others are in need is not a Godly attitude.

Read 2 Corinthians 8:16-17

Titus was eager to go to Corinth as Paul asked because his love for them and his excitement for the mission of giving to the poor was as strong as Paul's.

Read 2 Corinthians 8:18-21

Paul does not name the "brother" is who accompanied Titus, but he had been chosen by the churches to accompany Paul in the collection and distribution of the money for the poor because he was trusted. Paul says he is praised for his service to the gospel. They are doing all they can to ensure everything is above reproach and there is no cause for criticism, not only in God's eyes, but in the eyes of man.

Read 2 Corinthians 8:22-24

A second messenger is being sent with Titus who is known to those in Corinth, although he is not named here. He calls Titus his partner and co-worker, therefore representing him, and the other two are representing the churches and a glory to Christ. He asks that they show these men the love of Christ so everyone will understand why Paul is so proud of them. He has bragged about them and wants them to live up to his praise.

2 Corinthians – Chapter 9

The kingdom of God grows through Christians' desire to help others. By joining together with other believers to do God's work, we increase our unity and the kingdom. We are not commanded to give, but we are commanded to love. When you love someone, you want to give your time and attention and provide for his/her needs. Giving is how we prove our love.

Read 2 Corinthians 9:1-5

He is so sure of the love and generosity of the church in Corinth, Paul is sure they will give willingly. He reminds them of their commitment from a year ago and wants them to fulfill that commitment. He asks that they not disappoint him. He was holding them accountable so he wouldn't be embarrassed about his confidence in them. He also asks that they have the money ready when Titus and his fellow travelers arrive so it doesn't look like the Corinthians are being forced to give, but are giving out of love.

Read 2 Corinthians 9:6-9

Paul tells the people in Corinth not to allow a lack of faith keep them from giving freely and generously. Giving gladly is more important than the amount we give. He also reminds them they will reap what they sow. If they give generously, generosity will be given back to them. If they give sparingly, they will reap sparingly. Have faith that God will provide.

He then quotes Psalm 112:9 from the scriptures where David spoke of a man who feared God and loved his neighbor enough to give to him whatever he needed. This is used to remind them that he who gives generously to the poor obtains righteousness.

Read 2 Corinthians 9:10-11

The resources God give us should be used wisely. Paul uses the illustration of seed. These seeds should be cultivated to produce more crops. If we invest what God gives us toward doing His work, He will provide us even more to give.

Read 2 Corinthians 9:12-15

Giving can serve as an act of worship to God and inspire other's faith and thanksgiving.

When we help provide others their needs, they praise God and thank Him. They also say prayers for us in their hearts and blessings are bestowed because of these prayers. So in an attempt to help others, grace comes back to us through their prayers. As we bless others, we are blessed.

Paul teaches us that all Christians lives should be entwined with each other, depending on one another. We are family, caring for each other and supporting each other, and in doing so, we give honor to our Lord.

2 Corinthians – Chapter 10

Although most of the Corinthian believers sided with Paul, there were still some who opposed him by claiming he had no authority over them. Here Paul defends his ministry.

Read 2 Corinthians 10:1-2

Paul wrote with great confidence in his letters, but in person he was very meek. His docile manner gave the impression to some that he was weak and lacked conviction. He says they are judging him according to worldly standards.

Read 2 Corinthians 10:3-6

We, as Christians, do not use human methods to win our battles. We use the weapons of God, including prayer, faith, hope, love, scripture, and the Holy Spirit. These are powerful and effective if used properly. They can break down any arguments against God and tear down any walls Satan builds to keep people from finding the Lord. We may be tempted to use human methods by beating our chest to show our strength, but God's humble ways will prevail where man's methods fail.

Paul uses military terms because he views our fight against sin and Satan as warfare.

Read 2 Corinthians 10:7-9

Paul points out the obvious facts. If the Christians in Corinth consider they belong to Christ, that in itself gives him authority over them. If he hadn't brought the Good News to them and taught them about Jesus, they wouldn't have known Christ at all. His letters were not meant to intimidate them, but to help them grow in their knowledge and faith in Christ.

Read 2 Corinthians 10:10-11

The people were judging Paul by his appearance and ability to convince people through his speaking skills. Historians described Paul as a short stout man with a prominent nose and balding head, although in his earlier days he had curly hair. He was bow-legged and had blue eyes with heavy brows, possibly even a unibrow (the description at that time was "closed brow").

Paul was not considered an eloquent speaker. Greece was known for producing great orators who were persuasive, articulate, and powerful. Apparently some were judging Paul by comparing him to other speakers they had heard. Being a great preacher is not the first requirement of being a great leader. Even Moses and Jeremiah had problems with speaking, yet they were great leaders. Paul had obediently responded to God's call and introduced Christianity to the Roman empire. That was no small feat. Paul spoke with authoritative power and spoke the truth directly. Orators at that time were more eloquent with lots of theatrical swagger. Those orators were after the applause and money, but Paul was looking for results through changed lives, not profit or fame.

F.A.C.T.S.

Read 2 Corinthians 10:12-18

Comparing ourselves by the world's standards produces pride within us. But if we measure ourselves using God's standards, there is no basis for pride. Rather than compare ourselves to others, we should always ask ourselves how we are living up to what God wants from us. That is what Paul is pointing out here. How does our life, as a Christian, compare to Jesus Christ? We should always seek God's approval rather than the praise of humans.

Paul quotes Jeremiah 9:24 to emphasize his point; "Let the one who boasts boast in the Lord."

2 Corinthians – Chapter 11

Paul knew it was wrong to boast, but felt he had to in order to defend himself to his accusers. Several times in this letter, he talks about all he has done and endured, but calls himself a fool for doing so. It feels wrong to be boastful even though he has to in order to prove himself and his actions.

Read 2 Corinthians 11:1-4

The word 'virgin' here refers to those who are unaffected by false doctrine. They remain true to Christ alone. Just as Eve lost her focus by listening to the serpent, Christians can also have many distractions that threaten to derail our faith. We must not allow our lives to become overcrowded and confused, weakening our commitment and devotion to Christ.

There are many false teachings that seem to make sense. But if those teachings contradict God's Word, we need to ignore them and remain faithful to what the Bible tells us. We cannot be sidetracked by pretty speeches and smooth talk by people who appear to have authority. God's Word is our authoritative guide.

False teachers try to preach a Jesus other than God's Son, a spirit other than the Holy Spirit, and a different way of salvation than the Gospel. Anyone who teaches anything different from what God's Word says are being deceptive.

Read 2 Corinthians 11:5-6

Paul compares himself to those eloquent speakers who were servants of Satan. He admits he isn't a trained speaker, but he does have knowledge and speaks only the truth. A simple and clear presentation listeners can understand is of much greater value than pretty speeches full of untruths.

Read 2 Corinthians 11:7-9

The people of Corinth were no different in their thinking as most are today. The value of an orator was determined by how much they charged. A great speaker would charge a large sum for their services; a fair one would charge a little cheaper rate; and a poor speaker would not charge at all. Since Paul asked for no fee, it was assumed he was an amateur with little authority on his topic. But Paul didn't want to burden anyone by asking for financial help.

It is not wrong for preachers to be paid for their services. In Matthew (10:10), Jesus taught that those who minister for God should be supported by those to whom they minister.

The churches in Macedonia had supplied his needs even for him to go to Corinth. That trip had not benefitted the people in Macedonia, so Paul says it was as if he had robbed them in order to not burden the people in Corinth.

Read 2 Corinthians 11:10-12

Paul insists he will continue boasting in order to expose the false men masquerading as apostles.

Read 2 Corinthians 11:13-15

In one Jewish writing, the Apocalypse of Moses, the story of Eve's temptation includes Satan masquerading as an angel. Paul may have been referring to this story. Nothing is more deceitful than the prince of darkness disguising himself as an angel of light. These false teachers, much in the same way, claimed to represent Christ as servants of righteousness, blatantly lying.

Read 2 Corinthians 11:16-23

Paul is embarrassed to be bragging about himself. He becomes sarcastic here, saying he must be boastful because the people in Corinth obviously believe in such things because they are "so wise." But in doing so, he feels like an ungodly fool.

Again, he compares himself to what the false teachers were claiming. He is also a Hebrew, an Israelite, a descendent of Abraham, and a servant of Christ, even more so than they. He says he has worked harder and suffered more than those false teachers ever had because of his love and devotion to the truth. He continues to show his discomfort of having to boast his credentials in order to convince them of his sincerity.

Read 2 Corinthians 11:24-27

Paul continues to list the trials he has endured in his service for Christ.

Thirty-nine lashes was the maximum punishment allowed under Jewish law. Paul was judged and sentenced by the Jews for his activities as a Christian five times. As a Roman citizen, he was also imprisoned under Roman law and beaten with rods, which was illegal punishment for a Roman citizen. Many of the trials listed here are also recorded in the book of Acts. Since Paul wrote this letter during his third missionary journey, he had many more trials to come. Paul's point here was that he had sacrificed his life for the gospel, something the false teachers would never do.

Read 2 Corinthians 11:28-29

On top of his sufferings, he also carried the burden of worrying about the young churches, concerned that they were remaining true to the gospel he had taught them. He reminds them that he is human and feels weak at times and is tempted to sin.

Read 2 Corinthians 11:30-33

Here Paul says God is his witness that all he is telling them is true.

King Aretas was king of the Nabateans (Edomites) from 9 B.C. to A.D. 40 and had appointed a governor to oversee the Nabatean population in Damascus. The Jews had been able to enlist this governor to help capture Paul. Paul was able to escape by being lowered in a basket from a window in the city wall. He told this story as one more example of what he'd experienced in the name of Christ.

In order for us, as Christians, to know a false teacher from a righteous one, we must ask ourselves a few questions:

- Do their teachings confirm scripture, or contradict it?
- Does the teacher affirm that Jesus Christ is God who came into the world as a man to save people from their sins?
- Is the teacher's life-style consistent with Biblical morality?

And, of course, in order to answer these questions, we must have knowledge of scripture and the gospel. Thus one good reason for Bible studies.

2 Corinthians – Chapter 12

Paul begins this part of his letter by giving us a glimpse into one of his visions. He feels it is wrong for him to boast about himself, but not about his experiences such as this vision. He tells about his vision to show how he had been uniquely touched by God.

Read 2 Corinthians 12:1-2

Paul isn't sure if his visit to the third heaven was an out-of-body experience or an in-body one. He says only God knows what it was. This encounter happened fourteen years prior to him writing this letter. There is no other scripture referring to "the third heaven" in those exact words, but through careful study of other Hebrew words used in scripture, we can derive an idea of what Paul is talking about.

The Hebrew word for heavens is "shamayim," a plural form, meaning heights, or elevations. It is found in the first verse of the Bible (Genesis 1:1; 2:1). The Bible teaches in the beginning God created the heavens and the earth, he did not make another heaven after this time. The phrase "heavens and earth" are used to indicate the whole universe (Genesis 1:1; Jeremiah 23:24; Acts 17:24). According to the Jewish tradition from the Bible there were three heavens. All are attributed to God as the creator as said in Psalm 102:25 *"Of old You laid the foundation of the earth, and the heavens are the work of Your hands."*

There are several other words used in the Hebrew. The word "marom" is also used (Psalms 68:18; 93:4; 102:19) as equivalent to shamayim. The Hebrew "galgal," literally a "wheel," is translated as "heaven" or "whirlwind," depending on which translation, in Psalms 77:18. The Hebrew "shahak" is translated as sky (Deuteronomy 33:26; Job 37:18; Psalms 18:11), or in the plural, clouds or heavens (Job 35:5; 36:28; Psalms 68:34.)

The Bible speaks of three heavens. The first being our immediate atmosphere, the second is outer space as far as it stretches, and the third is the place where God himself dwells, or what Jesus called the "Father's house."

The first heaven is the earth's atmosphere, which is the immediate sky, where we see the "fowls of the heaven" (Genesis 2:19; 7:3,23; Psalms 8:8, etc.), and "the eagles of heaven" (Lamentations 4:19). It is our atmosphere that surrounds the earth.

Read Genesis 1:14

Read Genesis 7:11-12

Read Genesis 8:2

Read Deuteronomy 11:17

Read Deuteronomy 28:12

Read Psalm 78: 23-23

The first heaven consists of the clouds and the atmosphere, the heavens above us, until we come to the stars.

The second heaven is outer space, the starry heavens, where our atmosphere ends.

Read Deuteronomy 17:3

Read Jeremiah 8:2

Read Matthew 24:29

It is the heavens in which the sun, moon, and stars are fixed in orbit. The stars are seemingly endless and the distance between all of them is staggering.

Read Psalm 19:1

In ancient times people were in awe of the starry expanse. Today we know how immense this really is.

The Hebrew word "raqiya" is the place in which the sun, moon, stars, and constellations are fixed.

Read Genesis 1:17

Read Isaiah 40:22

Read Psalm 19:4,6

The third heaven is where God and the holy angels and creatures, and spirits of just men dwell. It is called "The heaven of heavens," (Deuteronomy 10:14; 1 Kings 8:27; Psalms 115:16; 148:4). (1Kings 8:27)

The third heaven is beyond the space and stars, where no man has seen by telescope. This heaven is the dwelling-place of God, to which Paul was taken, and whose wonders he was permitted to behold, this region where God dwells.

Read Hebrews 4:14

Jesus ascended to the place He was before He became man.

Read Hebrews 7:26

Jesus is more important than the dwelling place of God and angels.

Read Hebrews 8:1

As our high Priest, he "is seated at the right hand of the throne of the Majesty in the heavens."

Read 2 Corinthians 4:17

Read 2 Corinthians 5:1,2

Christ calls it his Father's house.

Read John 14:2

Read Luke 23:43

Heaven is the inheritance of all believers where there is fullness of joy, and everlasting blessedness; the place of our inheritance where Jesus went ahead to "prepare" for us that we may be with him.

Read 2 Corinthians 12:3-5

Paul explains he saw Paradise. We know that Jesus went to Paradise immediately at death. It is believed by some that Paradise is the place spirits go between their death and their resurrection; a place more glorious than earth, but not as glorious as the third heaven. Others believe Paradise and the third heaven are the same place and Paul is using the terms interchangeably.

Some believe the word "paradise," which occurs only three times in the New Testament (Luke 23:43; 2 Corinthians 12:4; Revelation 2:7), describes a different facet within the third heaven. This word occurs often in the Septuagint as the translation of the word garden; Genesis 2:8-10,15-16; 3:1-3,8,16,23-24; 13:10; Numbers 24:6; Isaiah 51:3; Ezekiel 28:13; 31:8-9; Joel 2:3; Isaiah 1:30; and Jeremiah 29:5. The Garden of Eden was referred to as Paradise.

NOTE: The Septuagint is a Greek translation of the Hebrew Bible made in the 3rd and 2nd centuries BC to meet the needs of Greek speaking Jews outside Palestine.

Paul says he heard things he could not tell. The English translation says he is *not permitted* to tell, but it could be that it is impossible for him to tell because there is no human language or comprehension for those things. Imagine a person who was born blind trying to explain the concept of color. God had allowed Paul to see heaven, yet it was either forbidden for him to tell others, or he could not find the words to explain it. The purpose of the vision was not so he could tell of heaven's glory, but so Paul would have a stronger conviction to continue his special mission and have the strength to endure the sufferings he would face.

Read 2 Corinthians 12:6-7

We do not know what the thorn in his flesh was, but there are several references to his affliction which seem to point to poor eyesight. Fourteen years before this epistle, Paul went to Galatia on his first missionary journey. Galatians 4:13-15 describes him as having a physical affliction so offensive in appearance that people didn't want to look at him. It says they would have given their own eyes. Why eyes, unless that was his particular need?

A disease of the eyes known as Chronic Ophthalmia was not extremely painful, but was repulsive in appearance. Maybe this was Paul's affliction. Also in Galatians 6:11 he mentions his large handwriting, which may have been due to poor eyesight.

Read 2 Corinthians 12:8-10

His affliction could have been epilepsy, malaria, an eye disease, or numerous other things. Whatever it was, he prayed for God to remove it so it didn't hinder his ability to spread the gospel. But God refused to remove it so Paul would remain humble and fight through the pain and humiliation. Those around him would see God working in his life through his continued devotion to his mission in spite of his affliction. This tenacity caused others to respect him more.

It is important to notice here that Paul does not accuse God of giving him this ailment. He makes it clear it was initiated by Satan to hinder his mission for Christ, but God used it to make him stronger and more effective as His witness.

Sometimes when we are given trials to endure, God uses us to teach others about the strength He can give us through our faith in Him. He also may use our afflictions to show others how fortunate they are. We should contemplate the trials of others when we are tempted to grumble about the small stuff in life that annoys us and rely on God to show us how to use our weaknesses more effectively. Our weaknesses help us develop character, deepens our worship, and in admitting our weakness, we affirm God's strength. It is through Him we can do all things, not simply on our own energy, effort, or talent. When we try to do God's work on our own, pride can intervene. When we allow God to fill us with His power, we are stronger than we could ever be on our own. That is why Paul took pleasure in his weaknesses.

When we are weak in ourselves, then we are strong in the grace of our Lord.

Read 2 Corinthians 12:11-13

Paul was hurt when the Corinthian church members and leaders doubted and questioned him. His boasting was not to satisfy his ego, but to defend himself as a messenger for Christ. He had done more for the Corinthian church than he had for any other of the churches. He had never asked them to feed and house him as he had other churches. He is being sarcastic when he says "Forgive me this wrong!" He is mockingly saying "Pardon me for not being a burden to you!"

Read 2 Corinthians 12:14-15

Paul loved the church in Corinth as a parent loves a child. He had founded it during his first visit and had returned to check on them since. He was now planning a third visit, but makes it clear he only wants to see them and teach them, not have them provide for him. He spared their purses to save their souls.

Read 2 Corinthians 12:16-18

Some of the doubters in the church in Corinth had called Paul crafty or devious, saying he had somehow tricked them and made money off of them. He is again being sarcastic when he refers to himself as a crafty fellow, using their words. He is incredulous that they could say such things when everything he had done was for their enlightenment, and he had not taken anything from them. He had even instructed Titus and his fellow traveler to not take anything from them when they had visited.

Read 2 Corinthians 12:19-21

Since they are saying such things about him, Paul is fearful they have fallen back into their old evil ways, allowing the outside influences to invade the church. He is concerned there may be a disparity between what he expects from them and what they expect from him when he visits. By listing his fears of what they have become, he hopes they will clean up their act before he arrives.

"Those who aim at clothing themselves with the fleece of the flock, and take no care of the sheep, are hirelings, and not good shepherds." (taken from "The NIV Matthew Henry Commentary in One Volume, Harper Collins Publishers, © 1992)

We should be like a candle, which consumes itself to give light to others.

2 Corinthians – Chapter 13

Paul dealt with ongoing problems within the Corinthian church. He could have ignored them and let them clean up their own conflicts, but he loved them enough to reach out to them with the love of Christ. Sometimes we must confront those we care about when they are ruining their lives with sin. Reports of sinfulness within the church had come to Paul causing him to write this letter. He wants to be careful that he doesn't accuse anyone based on one report.

In Deuteronomy 19, Moses expanded on the ten commandments to express the duties of righteousness between man and man. In verse 15, he relates to the ninth commandment, "You shall not give false witness."

Read Deuteronomy 19:15

In the beginning of chapter 13, Paul refers to this Old Testament scripture.

Read 2 Corinthians 13:1-3

Paul repeats a warning he had given them during his second visit. He warns that when he returns he will not be tolerant toward those who have sinned and not repented. Some of the customary ways of handling such unrepentance in the early church included confronting the accused and publicly denouncing their behavior; then exercise church discipline by calling them before the church leaders and possibly excommunicating them from the church.

Read 2 Corinthians 13:4-6

God gives us strength to do things we normally might find difficult. Paul doesn't want to discipline those he loves within the Corinthian church, but feels it is his duty as their spiritual leader. Just as we get physical checkups, Paul urged the Corinthians to give themselves a spiritual checkup; to examine themselves to see if they really were Christians by testing their faithfulness. Once again Paul points at himself as the example they should follow, not those false teachers who were infiltrating the church and trying to lead them astray.

Read 2 Corinthians 13:7-9

Parents want their children to grow into mature adults. In the same way, Paul wanted the Corinthians to grow into mature believers. He didn't want them to depend on him to be their example all their lives, but for them to grow strong in their faith so they could do what was right on their own.

Read 2 Corinthians 13:10

Paul's goal was to encourage them. He did not want to discipline them. He hoped his letter would have the desired effect so when he arrived they would be repentant and living lives full of faith.

Read 2 Corinthians 13:11-14

As he closes his letter, he wants to leave them with positive advice to help them face the needs of their church. He told them to aim for perfection, and be there for each other by coming together in peace. If Christians will concentrate on what they have in common, the one thing that bonds them as Christians—God's love and grace—and avoid the pitfalls of disagreements, they will be able to solve problems together and accomplish the work Jesus asks of us.

Paul's farewell blessing invokes all three members of the Trinity. Although the word 'Trinity' is not explicitly used in scripture, verses such as this show it was believed and experienced through knowing God's peace, love, and fellowship.

BIBLIOGRAPHY
(F.A.C.T.S. Sources of Information)

The NIV Study Bible Copyright© 1985 by The Zondervan Corporation
Scripture taken from the Holy Bible, New International Version Copyright© 1973, 1978, 1984 International Bible Society. Used by permission of Zondervan Bible Publishers.

New American Standard Bible – The Student Bible
Scripture taken from the New American Standard Bible®, Copyright©1960, 1962, 1963, 1968, 1971, 1972, 1973, 1975, 1977, 1995 by The Lockman Foundation. Used by permission.

The Life Application Study Bible, New International Version edition
Scripture taken from the Holy Bible, New International Version®NIV®, Copyright© 1973, 1978, 1984 by International Bible Society. Used by permission of Zondervan Publishing House. All rights reserved.

The 1599 Geneva Bible Copyright© 2006-2010 by Tolle Lege Press

The Holy Bible Old and New Testaments in the King James Version Copyright©1976 by Thomas Nelson, Inc.

Halley's Bible Handbook® Copyright© 1965 Zondervan Publishing House, Halley's Bible Handbook® Inc.

Illustrated Dictionary & Concordance of the Bible Copyright© 1986 by G.G. The Jerusalem Publishing House LTD.

The New Strong's Expanded Dictionary of Bible Words / James Strong, LL.D., S.T.D. Copyright© 2001 by Thomas Nelson Publishers

Who's Who in the Bible by Joan Comay and Ronald Browning Copyright© MCMLXXI, 1980 edition published by Bonanza Books, distributed by Crown Publishers, Inc.

The World Book Encyclopedia Copyright© 1985 by World Book, Inc.

A Newcomer's Guide to the Bible: Themes and Time Lines / Michael C. Armour; Copyright© 1999 College Press Publishing Company Fourth Printing 2003

The NIV Matthew Henry Commentary in One Volume Copyright© 1992 by Harper Collins Publishers Ltd.

Notes taken from various sermons, homilies, Bible studies, and discussions through the years from pastors, preachers, and ministers including, but not limited to, the following: Rev. David Pruitt • Rev. Thomas Farmer • Dr. T.A. Powell • Minister G. Harrison (Harry) Swain • Rev. Herman Dowdy • Minister Bill McCracken • Pastor Rick Phillips • Minister David Jones • Dr. Fred Scaggs • Minister Gary Jones • Rev. Keith Reynolds • Minister Ronnie Jones • Pastor Steve Via • Minister Bill Wines • Pastor Todd Combee • Evangelist E.L. Jones • Rev. Rebekah Johns • Rev. Sylvester H. Bullock • Rev. Beverly Bullock • Rev. Dr. Paul Flowers

F.A.C.T.S.

The aforementioned sources were studied and notes were taken and used to understand the period in which the scriptures were written as well as to understand the meaning of the words based on the letter writer's intent at that time. Unless otherwise noted, any instance where the words are identical to any of the sources is purely accidental.

ABOUT THE AUTHOR

Joanne Liggan is a novelist, public speaker and writing instructor, and founder of the Hanover Writers Club and the Hanover Book Festival. Her family saga trilogy includes *Heir of Deception*, *Air of Truth*, and *Err At Sea*.

After being reared in a Christian home and accepting Christ at a young age, Liggan developed a thirst for Biblical knowledge as a young adult and has spent her life researching various denominations and studying the scriptures. Her spiritual journey has not always been smooth, but rather a very bumpy flight at times. Researching different belief systems can cause confusion and raise questions, but her determination to seek the truth through scripture sustained her core beliefs and led her to write this series of study guides.

To learn more about Joanne, you may visit her website at www.liggan.net.